MATHS
PUZZLES
AND
GAMES

for ages 9-11

Andrew
Brodie

Contents

Introduction

Maths, Puzzles and Games 9-11 contains a wide range of puzzles and games that promote mathematical skills and logical thinking. Most of the activities are easy to administer and each of them will form a valuable element of a maths lesson. Each puzzle or game sheet features brief teacher's notes, which include a suggested objective.

The puzzles provide practice in a range of mental arithmetic skills and knowledge, such as revising addition, subtraction, multiplication and division facts, doubling, halving, adding two-digit numbers mentally, etc. Some children will solve some of the puzzles quite quickly, whilst others may take longer and may need extra support. In each case, encourage the children to follow logical steps to solve the puzzle. Once they can follow the patterns and relationships featured in a particular type of puzzle, give them further puzzles of this type to consolidate their understanding.

Games such as bingo can help the children gain some fundamental skills in an atmosphere of fun informality. Many children in the 9-11 age range still struggle with place value, so, for example, thousands bingo, decimals bingo and number variety bingo games can provide a focus for discussion as well as repeated exposure to the place value patterns.

THE CD-ROM

All of the activities are included on the accompanying CD-ROM to enable you to display them on the whiteboard for discussion purposes. You might prefer to print the sheets directly from the CD-ROM rather than to photocopy them from the book. Answers to all the puzzles are also provided on the CD-ROM.

Further mental maths puzzles can be found in our titles Maths Mindstretchers for Ages 7-9 and Maths Mindstretchers for Ages 9-11.

Guidelines for assessing mathematics

You could use these pages as individual record sheets by highlighting the statements when you feel that pupils are secure in the specific skills that these represent.

Level 3

Using and applying mathematics

Pupils try different approaches and find ways of overcoming difficulties that arise when they are solving problems. They are beginning to organise their work and check results. Pupils discuss their mathematical work and are beginning to explain their thinking. They use and interpret mathematical symbols and diagrams. Pupils show that they understand a general statement by finding particular examples that match it.

- Do the children select the mathematics they use in a wider range of classroom activities? For example: Do they use classroom discussions to break into a problem, recognising similarities to previous work? Do they put the problem into their own words? Do they use mathematical content from levels 2 and 3? Do they choose their own equipment appropriate to the task, including calculators? ❏

- Do they try different approaches and find ways of overcoming difficulties that arise when they are solving problems? For example: Do they check their work and make appropriate corrections? Are they beginning to look for patterns in results as they work and do they use these to find other possible outcomes? (Ma1 Level 3) ❏

- Are the children beginning to organise their work and check results? For example: Are they beginning to develop their own ways of recording? Do they develop an organised approach as they get into recording their work on a problem? ❏

- Do they discuss their mathematical work and begin to explain their thinking? Do they use appropriate mathematical vocabulary? Do they talk about their findings by referring to their written work? ❏

- Do they use and interpret mathematical symbols and diagrams? (Ma1 Level 3) ❏

- Do the children understand a general statement by finding particular examples that match it? For example: Can they make a generalisation, with the assistance of probing questions and prompts? ❏

- Do they review their work and reasoning? For example: Do they respond to 'What if?' questions? When they have solved a problem, can they pose a similar problem for a partner? (Ma1 Level 3) ❏

Number

Pupils show understanding of place value in numbers up to 1000 and use this to make approximations. They begin to use decimal notation and to recognise negative numbers, in contexts such as money and temperature. Pupils use mental recall of addition and subtraction facts to 20 in solving problems involving larger numbers. They add and subtract numbers with two digits mentally and numbers with three digits using written methods. They use mental recall of the 2, 3, 4, 5 and 10 multiplication tables and derive the associated division facts. They solve whole number problems involving multiplication or division, including those that give rise to remainders. They use simple fractions that are several parts of a whole and recognise when two simple fractions are equivalent.

- Do the children understand place value in numbers to 1000? For example: Do they represent/ compare numbers using number lines, 100 squares, base 10 materials, etc? Do they recognise that some numbers can be represented as different arrays? Do they use understanding of place value to multiply/divide whole numbers by 10 (whole number answers)? ❏

- Can the children use place value to make approximations? Do they recognise negative numbers in contexts such as temperature? Do they recognise a wider range of sequences, e.g. recognise sequences of multiples of 2, 5 and 10? (Ma2 Level 3) ❏

Andrew Brodie: Maths Puzzles and Games 9–11 © A&C Black 2011

- Do the children use simple fractions that are several parts of a whole and recognise when two simple fractions are equivalent? Do they understand and use unit fractions such as $\frac{1}{2}, \frac{1}{4}, \frac{1}{3}, \frac{1}{5}, \frac{1}{10}$ and find those fractions of shapes and sets of objects? Do they recognise and record fractions that are several parts of the whole, such as $\frac{3}{4}, \frac{2}{5}$? Do they recognise some fractions that are equivalent to $\frac{1}{2}$? ❏

- Are they beginning to use decimal notation in contexts such as money? For example: Can they order decimals with one decimal place or two decimal places in the context of money? Do they know that £3.06 equals 306p? (Ma2 Level 3) ❏

- Can the children derive associated division facts from known multiplication facts? Do they use inverses to find missing whole numbers in problems such as 'I think of a number, double it and add 5. The answer is 35. What was my number?'? ❏

- Are the children beginning to understand the role of the equals sign? For example: Can they solve 'balancing' problems such as $7 \times 10 = 82 - \boxed{}$? (Ma2 Level 3) ❏

- Can the children add and subtract two-digit numbers mentally? Can they use mental recall of the 2, 3, 4, 5 and 10 multiplication tables? Are they beginning to know multiplication facts for the 6, 7, 8 and 9 multiplication tables? (Ma2 Level 3) ❏

- Can the children use mental recall of addition and subtraction facts to 20 in solving problems involving larger numbers? Do they solve whole number problems including those involving multiplication or division that may give rise to remainders? (Ma2 Level 3) ❏

- Can the children add and subtract three-digit numbers using a written method? Can they multiply and divide two-digit numbers by 2, 3, 4, 5 or 10 with whole number answers and remainders? (Ma2 Level 3) ❏

Shape, space and measures

Pupils classify 3-D and 2-D shapes in various ways using mathematical properties such as reflective symmetry for 2-D shapes. They use non-standard units, standard metric units of length, capacity and mass, and standard units of time, in a range of contexts.

- Can the children classify 3-D and 2-D shapes in various ways using mathematical properties such as reflective symmetry for 2-D shapes? Do they sort objects and shapes using more than one criterion? Are they beginning to understand the terms regular and irregular? Do they recognise right angles in shapes in different orientations? Do they recognise angles that are bigger or smaller than 90°? Are they beginning to use the terms acute and obtuse? Do they recognise right-angled and equilateral triangles? Can they demonstrate that a shape has reflectional symmetry by folding? Do they recognise when a shape does not have a line of symmetry? Can they recognise common 3-D shapes? Can they relate 3-D shapes to drawings and photographs of them? Are they beginning to recognise nets of familiar 3-D shapes? (Ma3 Level 3) ❏

- Do the children recognise shapes in different orientations? Can they reflect shapes, presented on a grid, in a vertical or horizontal mirror line? Are they beginning to reflect simple shapes in a mirror line presented at 45°? Can they describe position and movement using terms such as left/right, clockwise/anticlockwise, quarter turn/90°? (Ma3 Level 3) ❏

- Do the children use non-standard units and standard metric units of length, capacity and mass in a range of contexts? For example: Can they measure a length to the nearest $\frac{1}{2}$ cm? Can they read simple scales? ❏

- Do they use standard units of time? Can they read a 12-hour clock and calculate time durations that do not go over the hour? ❏

- Do they use a wider range of measures? For example: Are they beginning to understand area as a measure of surface and perimeter as a measure of length? Are they beginning to find areas of shapes by counting squares? Do they recognise angles as a measure of turn and know that one whole turn is 360 degrees? (Ma3 Level 3) ❏

Handling data

Pupils extract and interpret information presented in simple tables and lists. They construct bar charts and pictograms, where the symbol represents a group of units, to communicate information they have gathered, and the interpret information presented in these forms.

- Can the children gather information by deciding what data to collect to answer a question and making appropriate choices for recording information? Can they construct bar charts and pictograms, where the symbol represents a group of units? Do they decide how best to present data, e.g. whether a bar chart, a pictogram or a Venn diagram would show the information most clearly? Can they decide upon an appropriate scale for a graph? Do they use Venn and Carroll diagrams to record their sorting and classifying of information? (Ma4 Level 3) ❑

- Can the children extract and interpret information presented in simple tables, lists, bar charts or pictograms? Can they use a key to interpret data? Can they read scales labelled in twos, fives and tens, including reading between labelled divisions? Can they compare data? Can they respond to questions of a more complex nature such as 'How many children took part in this survey altogether?'? Can they understand the idea of certain and impossible relating to probability in the context of data regarding everyday situations? (Ma4 Level 3) ❑

Andrew Brodie: Maths Puzzles and Games 9–11 © A&C Black 2011

Level 4

Using and applying mathematics

Pupils are developing their own strategies for solving problems and are using these strategies both in working within mathematics and in applying mathematics to practical contexts. They present information and results in a clear and organised way. They search for a solution by trying out ideas of their own.

- Do the children develop their own strategies for solving problems? Do they make their own suggestions of ways to tackle a range of problems? Do they make connections to previous work? Do they pose and answer questions related to a problem? Do they check answers and ensure solutions make sense in the context of the problem? Do they review their work and approaches? ❑

- Do the children use their own strategies within mathematics and in applying mathematics to practical context? Do they use mathematical content from Levels 3 and 4 to solve problems and investigate? (Ma1 Level 4) ❑

- Do the children present information and results in a clear and organised way? Do they organise their written work, e.g. recording results in order? Do they begin to work in an organised way from the start? Do they consider appropriate units? Do they use related vocabulary accurately? (Ma1 Level 4) ❑

- Do the children search for a solution by trying out ideas of their own? Do they check their methods and justify answers? Do they identify patterns as they work and form their own generalisations/rules in words? ❑

Number

Pupils use their understanding of place value to multiply and divide whole numbers by 10 or 100. In solving number problems, pupils use a range of mental methods of computation with the four operations, including mental recall of multiplication facts up to 10 x 10 and quick derivation of corresponding division facts. They use efficient written methods of addition and subtraction and of short multiplication and division. They add and subtract decimals to two places and order decimals to three places. In solving problems with or without a calculator, pupils check the reasonableness of their results by reference to the knowledge of the context or to the size of the numbers. They recognise approximate proportions of a whole and use simple fractions and percentages to describe these. Pupils recognise and describe number patterns, and relationships including multiple, factor and square. They begin to use simple formulae expressed in words. Pupils use and interpret coordinates in the first quadrant.

- Do the children recognise and describe number patterns, e.g. continuing sequences involving decimals? Do they recognise and describe number relationships, including multiple, factor and square? Do they use place value to multiply and divide whole numbers by 10 or 100? (Ma2 Level 4) ❑

- Do the children recognise approximate proportions of a whole and use simple fractions and percentages to describe these? Do they recognise simple equivalence between fractions, decimals and percentages, e.g. $\frac{1}{2}, \frac{1}{4}, \frac{1}{10}, \frac{3}{4}$? Can they convert mixed numbers to improper fractions and vice versa? Can they order decimals to three decimal places? Are they beginning to understand simple ratio? (Ma2 Level 4) ❑

- Can the pupils use inverse operations, e.g. use a calculator and inverse operations to find missing numbers, including decimals? Can they 'undo' two-step problems? Do they understand 'balancing sums' including those using division? Do they understand the use of brackets in simple calculations? Can they quickly derive division facts that correspond to multiplication facts up to 10×10? (Ma2 Level 4) ❑

- Do the children use a range of mental methods of computation with all operations, e.g. calculate complements to 1000? Do they recall multiplication facts up to 10×10 and quickly derive corresponding division facts, e.g. use their knowledge of tables and place value in calculations with multiples of 10? Can they use efficient written methods of addition and subtraction and of short multiplication and division? Can they add and subtract decimals to two places? Can they multiply a simple decimal by a single digit? (Ma2 Level 4) ❑

- Can the children solve problems with or without a calculator? Can they solve two-step problems choosing appropriate operations? Can they deal with two constraints simultaneously? Can they interpret a calculator display correctly in the context of money? Can they carry out simple calculations involving negative numbers in context? Do they check the reasonableness of results with reference to the context or size of numbers? (Ma2 Level 4) ❏

- Are the children beginning to use simple formulae expressed in words? Can they use and interpret coordinates in the first quadrant? (Ma2 Level 4) ❏

Shape, space and measures

Pupils make 3-D mathematical models by linking given faces or edges, draw common 2-D shapes in different orientations on grids. They reflect simple shapes in a mirror line. They choose and use appropriate units and measurements, interpreting, with appropriate accuracy, numbers on a range of measuring instruments. They find perimeters of simple shapes and find areas by counting squares.

- Can the children use the properties of 2-D and 3-D shapes, e.g. can they recognise and name most quadrilaterals? Can they recognise right-angled, equilateral, isosceles and scalene triangles? Can they recognise an oblique line of symmetry in a shape? Do they use mathematical terms such as horizontal, vertical, congruent? Do they understand properties of shapes, e.g. why a square is a special rectangle? Do they visualise shapes and recognise them in different orientations? Can they make 3-D models by linking given faces or edges? (Ma3 Level 4) ❏

- Can the children draw common 2-D shapes in different orientations on grids, e.g. complete a rectangle which has two sides drawn at an oblique angle to the grid? Can they reflect simple shapes in a mirror line, e.g. use a grid to plot the reflection in a mirror line presented at 45°? Can they rotate a simple shape or object about its centre or a vertex? Can they translate shapes horizontally or vertically? (Ma3 Level 4) ❏

- Do the pupils choose appropriate units and instruments? Do they interpret, with appropriate accuracy, numbers on a range of measuring instruments, e.g. measure a length using mm, to within 2mm? Do they measure and draw acute and obtuse angles to the nearest 5°, when one edge is horizontal/vertical? Do they find perimeters of simple shapes and find areas by counting squares and part squares? Are they beginning to find the areas of shapes that need to be divided into rectangles? Do they use 'number of squares in a row times number of rows' to find the area of a rectangle? Can they use units of time, e.g. read and interpret timetables? (Ma3 Level 4) ❏

Handling data

Pupils collect discrete data and record them using a frequency table. They understand and use the mode and range to describe sets of data. They group data, where appropriate, in equal class intervals, represent collected data in frequency diagrams and interpret such diagrams. They construct and interpret simple line graphs.

- Do the children collect discrete data? For example, given a problem, do they suggest possible answers and data to collect; do they test a hypothesis about the frequency of an event by collecting data? Do they group data, where appropriate, in equal class intervals? Do they record discrete data using a frequency table? (Ma4 Level 4) ❏

- Do the children represent collected data in frequency diagrams? Do the children construct simple line graphs? Do the children continue to use Venn and Carroll diagrams to record their sorting and classifying of information? (Ma4 Level 4) ❏

- Do the children understand and use the mode and range to describe sets of data? Can they interpret frequency diagrams and simple line graphs? Can they interpret simple pie charts? Can they interpret the scale on bar graphs and line graphs, reading between the labelled divisions? Can they interpret the total amount of data represented? Can they compare data sets and respond to questions? Do they understand the language of probability such as more likely, equally likely, fair, unfair, certain? (Ma4 Level 4) ❏

⑧

Level 5

Using and applying mathematics

Pupils identify and obtain necessary information in order to carry through tasks and solve mathematical problems. They check their results, considering whether these are sensible? Pupils show understanding of situations be describing them mathematically using symbols, words and diagrams. They draw simple conclusions of their own and give an explanation of their reasoning.

- Do the pupils identify and obtain necessary information to carry through a task and solve mathematical problems? Do they recognise information that is important to solving the problem, determine what is missing and develop lines of enquiry? Can they break a several-step problem or investigation into simpler steps? Do they consider efficient methods, relating problems to previous experiences? Do they check results, considering whether these are reasonable? Do they solve word problems and investigations from a range of contexts? (Ma1 Level 5) ❑

- Do the pupils show understanding of situations by describing them mathematically using symbols, words and diagrams? Do they organise their work from the outset, looking for ways to record systematically? Do they decide how best to represent conclusions, using appropriate recording? Are they beginning to understand and use formulae and symbols to represent problems? (Ma1 Level 5) ❑

- Do the pupils draw simple conclusions of their own and give an explanation of their reasoning? ❑

Number

Pupils use their understanding of place value to multiply and divide whole numbers and decimals by 10, 100 or 1000. They order, add and subtract negative numbers in context. They use all four operations with decimals to two places. They reduce a fraction to its simplest form by cancelling common factors and solve simple problems involving ratio and direct proportion. They calculate fractional or percentage parts of quantities and measurements, using a calculator where appropriate. Pupils understand and use an appropriate non-calculator method for solving problems that involve multiplying and dividing any three-digit number by any two-digit number. They check their solutions by applying inverse operations or estimating using approximations. They construct, express in symbolic form, and use simple formulae involving one or two operations. They use brackets appropriately. Pupils use and interpret coordinates in all four quadrants.

- Do the pupils use understanding of place value to multiply and divide whole numbers and decimals by 10, 100 or 1000? Can they explain the effect? Can they round decimals to the nearest decimal place? Can they order negative numbers in context? Do they recognise and use number patterns and relationships? (Ma2 Level 5) ❑

- Can the pupils use equivalence between fractions? Can they reduce a fraction to its simplest form by cancelling common factors? Can they order fractions and decimals? Do they understand simple ratio? (Ma2 Level 5) ❑

- Do the pupils use known facts, place value and knowledge of operations to calculate? Can they calculate decimal complements to 10 or 100? Can they use known facts to multiply a two-digit number by a single digit? Can they calculate simple fractions or percentages of a number or quantity? Can they apply inverse operations? Can they use brackets appropriately? Do they know and use the order of operations, including brackets? (Ma2 Level 5) ❑

- Can the pupils add and subtract negative numbers in context? Can they estimate using approximations? Can they use all four operations with decimals to two places? Can they add and subtract numbers that do not have the same number of decimal places? Can they multiply or divide decimal numbers by a single digit? Can they use a calculator where appropriate to calculate fractions/percentages of quantities or measurements? Do they understand and use an appropriate non-calculator method for solving problems that involve multiplying and dividing any three-digit number by any two-digit number? (Ma2 Level 5) ❑

- Can the pupils solve simple problems involving ordering, adding or subtracting negative numbers in context? Can they solve simple problems involving ratio and direct proportion? Do they approximate to check answers to problems are of the correct magnitude? Do they check solutions by applying inverse operations or by estimating using approximations? (Ma2 Level 5) ❏

- Can the pupils construct, express in symbolic form, and use simple formulae involving one or two operations? Can they evaluate expressions by substituting numbers into them? Do they use symbols to represent an unknown number or a variable? Can they use and interpret coordinates in all four quadrants? (Ma2 Level 5) ❏

Shape, space and measures

Pupils measure and draw angles to the nearest degree, and use language associated with angle, when constructing models and when drawing or using shapes. Pupils know the angle sum of a triangle and that of angles at a point. They identify all the symmetries of 2-D shapes. The know the rough metric equivalents of imperial units still in daily use and convert one metric unit to another. They make sensible estimates of a range of measures in relation to everyday situations. Pupils understand and use the formula for the area of a rectangle.

- Do the pupils understand 'parallel' and are they beginning to understand 'perpendicular'? Can they classify quadrilaterals, including trapezium and kite, using their properties? Do they know and use the angle sum of a triangle and that of angles at a point? (Ma3 Level 5) ❏

- Can the pupils identify all the symmetries of 2-D shapes? Can the pupils transform shapes by reflection, rotation or translation? (Ma3 Level 5) ❏

- Can the pupils measure and draw lines to the nearest degree? Can they construct a triangle given the length of two sides and the angle between them? Do they use the language associated with angle? Can they interpret scales on a range of measuring instruments? Solve problems involving the conversion of units? Can they make sensible estimates of a range of measures in relation to everyday situations? Do they understand and use the formula for the area of a rectangle and distinguish area from perimeter? ❏

Handling data

Pupils understand and use the mean of discrete data. They compare two simple distributions, using the range and mode, median or mean. They interpret graphs and diagrams, including pie charts, and draw conclusions. They understand and use the probability scale from 0 to 1. Pupils find and justify probabilities, and approximations to these, by selecting and using methods based on equally likely outcomes and experimental evidence, as appropriate. They understand that different outcomes may result from repeating an experiment.

- Do the pupils ask questions, plan how to answer them and collect the data required? Do they understand that different outcomes may result from repeating an experiment? (Ma4 Level 5) ❏

- Can the pupils understand and use the mean? Can they understand and use the probability scale from 0 to 1? Can they find and justify probabilities and approximations to these? Can they create and interpret line graphs where the intermediate values have meaning? (Ma4 Level 5) ❏

- Can the pupils compare two simple distributions, using the range and the mode, median or mean? Can they interpret graphs and diagrams, including pie charts, and draw conclusions? (Ma4 Level 5) ❏

Name _____ Date _____

Can you play addition bingo?

26 + 14		32 + 29		45 + 37
	18 + 23	28 + 28		48 + 29
56 + 39	64 + 23		72 + 27	

27 + 33	19 + 26		35 + 42	
66 + 28		75 + 16		48 + 17
		64 + 29	53 + 28	35 + 35

	28 + 13	34 + 17		45 + 28
58 + 36	67 + 24		46 + 36	
53 + 27			67 + 27	75 + 21

24 + 19	18 + 32		46 + 54	22 + 29
39 + 39	65 + 16	55 + 24		
		82 + 17		66 + 32

Teacher's notes

Suggested objective: *Add two digit numbers to two digit numbers.*

These bingo cards should be used in conjunction with the number cards on sheet 14. Pupils match the addition that totals the number called. Pupils should also be supplied with some blank cards or counters to cover their numbers as they are called out. 'Bingo' is called out by a pupil when he makes a line.

Name _____ *Date* _____

Can you play addition bingo?

40	61	82	41
56	77	95	87
99	60	45	94
91	65	93	81
70	51	73	94
80	96	43	50
100	78	79	98

Teacher's notes

Suggested objective: *Add two digit numbers to two digit numbers.*

These number cards should be used in conjunction with the bingo cards on sheet 1. The caller will call out each number at random for pupils to match to a calculation on their bingo card.

Andrew Brodie: Maths Puzzles and Games 9–11 © A&C Black 2011

Name _____ Date _____

Can you play subtraction bingo?

	100 – 64	90 – 35		120 – 59
	130 – 48		110 – 56	92 – 36
71 – 25		84 – 69	65 –17	

100 – 32	80 – 27		120 – 43	130 – 62
	110 – 47	96 – 28		
	73 – 39		81 – 12	63 – 24

100 – 54		80 – 31		120 – 65
	130 – 86	110 – 62		83 – 77
	92 – 68		85 – 49	66 – 27

100 – 72	90 – 46		120 – 83	
130 – 74			110 – 73	91 – 32
	74 – 28	86 – 59	67 – 31	

Teacher's notes

Suggested objective: *Subtract two digit numbers from two or three digit numbers.*

These bingo cards should be used in conjunction with the number cards on sheet 4. Pupils match the subtraction that totals the number called. Pupils should also be supplied with some blank cards or counters to cover their numbers as they are called out. 'Bingo' is called out by a pupil when he makes a line.

Can you play subtraction bingo?

36	55	61	82
54	56	46	15
48	53	77	68
63	34	69	39
49	44	6	24
28	37	59	27

Teacher's notes

Suggested objective: *Subtract two digit numbers from two or three digit numbers.*

These number cards should be used in conjunction with the bingo cards on sheet 3. The caller will call out each number at random for pupils to match to a calculation on their bingo card.

Name _____ *Date* _____

Can you play multiplication bingo?

		6×9		7×8
2×8	3×9		4×6	5×5
	6×7	8×4	9×9	

2×8		3×7	4×8	
	5×10	6×2		7×8
9×6		8×5		9×4

3×4		5×7	6×8	7×9
	5×8		3×9	
2×6		6×10		5×4

4×6	7×8		9×2	
7×10			5×6	8×6
4×9		3×8		6×7

Teacher's notes

Suggested objective: *Recall quickly multiplication facts up to 10 × 10.*

These bingo cards should be used in conjunction with the number cards on sheet 6. Pupils match the multiplication that totals the number called. Pupils should also be supplied with some blank cards or counters to cover their numbers as they are called out. 'Bingo' is called out by a pupil when he makes a line.

Name _____ Date _____

Can you play multiplication bingo?

56	54	16	27
24	25	42	32
81	21	50	12
40	36	35	48
63	60	20	18
70	30		

Teacher's notes

Suggested objective: *Recall quickly multiplication facts up to 10 × 10.*

These number cards should be used in conjunction with the bingo cards on sheet 5. The caller will call out each number at random for pupils to match to a calculation on their bingo card.

Andrew Brodie: Maths Puzzles and Games 9–11 © A&C Black 2011

Name _____ **Date** _____

Can you play division bingo?

56 ÷ 8		81 ÷ 9		40 ÷ 5
40 ÷ 4		30 ÷ 6	42 ÷ 7	
72 ÷ 4		80 ÷ 4		64 ÷ 4

21 ÷ 7		35 ÷ 5	40 ÷ 8	
	36 ÷ 6			16 ÷ 4
63 ÷ 7	96 ÷ 3	78 ÷ 3	63 ÷ 3	

20 ÷ 4		28 ÷ 7	36 ÷ 3	
42 ÷ 6			54 ÷ 9	64 ÷ 8
	100 ÷ 5	75 ÷ 5	90 ÷ 5	

42 ÷ 6	54 ÷ 6		60 ÷ 5	
	18 ÷ 9		25 ÷ 5	
56 ÷ 7	120 ÷ 2	84 ÷ 2		90 ÷ 2

Teacher's notes

Suggested objective: *Recall quickly multiplication facts up to 10 × 10 and derive quickly corresponding division facts.*

These bingo cards should be used in conjunction with the number cards on sheet 8. Pupils match the division that totals the number called. Pupils should also be supplied with some blank cards or counters to cover their numbers as they are called out. 'Bingo' is called out by a pupil when he makes a line.

Name _____ Date _____

Can you play division bingo?

7	9	8	10
5	6	18	20
16	3	4	32
26	31	12	15
2	60	42	45

Teacher's notes

Suggested objective: *Recall quickly multiplication facts up to 10 × 10 and derive quickly corresponding division facts.*

These bingo cards should be used in conjunction with the bingo cards on sheet 7.

9

Name _____ Date _____

Can you play multiplication pairs?

4×7	5×7	6×7	7×7
8×7	9×7	4×8	5×8
6×8	8×8	9×8	3×9
4×9	5×9	6×9	9×9

Teacher's notes

Suggested objective: *Can you play multiplication pairs?*

These cards should be used in conjunction with the answer cards on sheet 10.
Note that the multiplication facts are the more difficult facts from the 7, 8 and 9 times tables. The children should cut out the cards from both worksheets then lay them out in four rows of eight cards. They then take turns to turn over a pair of cards. If the answer matches the question they can keep the card and have another go. If the cards don't match they should be replaced where they were – do the children remember where certain cards are?

Andrew Brodie: Maths Puzzles and Games 9–11 © A&C Black 2011

Name _____ Date _____

Can you play multiplication pairs?

28	35	42	49
56	63	32	40
48	64	72	27
36	45	54	81

Teacher's notes

Suggested objective: *Recall quickly multiplication facts from the 7, 8 and 9 times tables.*

These cards should be used in conjunction with the question cards on sheet 9.
Note that the multiplication facts are the more difficult facts from the 7, 8 and 9 times tables. The children should cut out the cards from both worksheets then lay them out in four rows of eight cards. They then take turns to turn over a pair of cards. If the answer matches the question they can keep the card and have another go. If the cards don't match they should be replaced where they were – do the children remember where certain cards are?

Andrew Brodie: Maths Puzzles and Games 9-11 © A&C Black 2011

Name _____ *Date* _____

Can you play division pairs?

81 ÷ 9	72 ÷ 9	63 ÷ 9	54 ÷ 9
45 ÷ 9	36 ÷ 9	64 ÷ 8	56 ÷ 8
48 ÷ 8	40 ÷ 8	32 ÷ 8	24 ÷ 8
49 ÷ 7	42 ÷ 7	35 ÷ 7	28 ÷ 7

Teacher's notes

Suggested objective: *Can you play division pairs?*

These cards should be used in conjunction with the answer cards on sheet 12.
Note that the division facts are the more difficult facts derived from the 7, 8 and 9 times tables. The children should cut out the cards from both worksheets then lay them out in four rows of eight cards. They then take turns to turn over a pair of cards. If the answer matches the question they can keep the card and have another go. If the cards don't match they should be replaced where they were – do the children remember where certain cards are?

Name _____ Date _____

Can you play division pairs?

9	8	7	6
5	4	8	7
6	5	4	3
7	6	5	4

Teacher's notes

Suggested objective: *Recall quickly division facts derived from the 7, 8 and 9 times tables.*

These cards should be used in conjunction with the question cards on sheet 11.

Note that the division facts are the more difficult facts derived from the 7, 8 and 9 times tables. The children should cut out the cards from both worksheets then lay them out in four rows of eight cards. They then take turns to turn over a pair of cards. If the answer matches the question they can keep the card and have another go. If the cards don't match they should be replaced where they were – do the children remember where certain cards are?

Name _____ *Date* _____

Can you follow the patterns?

Look at the diagram.

For every horizontal arrow (→) you must always add 6.

For every vertical arrow (↓) you must always add 8.

Write the missing numbers in the boxes.

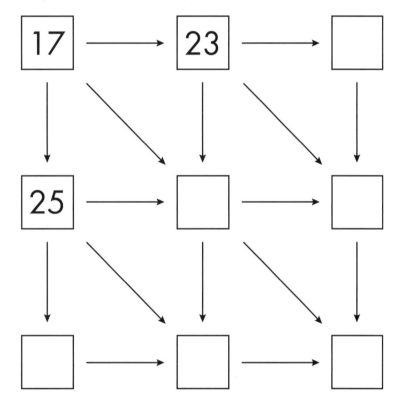

What addition could be written next to diagonal arrows like this (↘)? Write it in the diagram.

What addition would be written next to arrows like this (↗)?

Teacher's notes

Suggested objective: *Identify and use patterns, relationships and properties of numbers.*

This activity will provide practice in addition as well as in logical thinking. Can the pupils identify the relationship that each arrow represents? Some pupils will complete the puzzle very quickly, although many make mistakes in identifying what should be written next to the diagonal arrows. When you are confident that the pupils have completed the puzzle, extend the activity by asking them how many number sequences can be found on the diagram then to continue each of these sequences to beyond 100.

Name _____ *Date* _____

Can you follow the patterns?

Look at the diagram.

For every horizontal arrow (→) you must always add 8.

For every vertical arrow (↓) you must always add 9.

Write the missing numbers in the boxes.

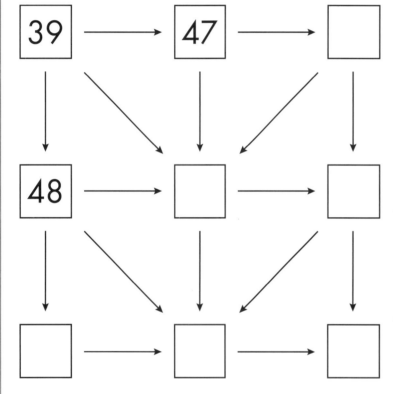

What addition could be written next to diagonal arrows like this (↘)? Write it in the diagram.

Why does this addition work?

_____

_____

What addition would be written next to arrows like this (↗)? Write it in the diagram.

Teacher's notes

Suggested objective: *Identify and use patterns, relationships and properties of numbers.*

This activity will provide practice in addition as well as in logical thinking. Can the pupils identify the relationship that each arrow represents? Some pupils will complete the puzzle very quickly, although many make mistakes in identifying what should be written next to the diagonal arrows. When you are confident that the pupils have completed the puzzle, extend the activity by asking them how many number sequences can be found on the diagram then to continue each of these sequences to beyond 100.

Andrew Brodie: Maths Puzzles and Games 9–11 © A&C Black 2011

Name _____ *Date* _____

Can you find and follow the patterns?

Look at the diagram.

For every horizontal arrow (→) you must always add the same number. Find the number.

For every vertical arrow (↓) you must always add the same number. Find the number.

Write the missing numbers in the boxes.

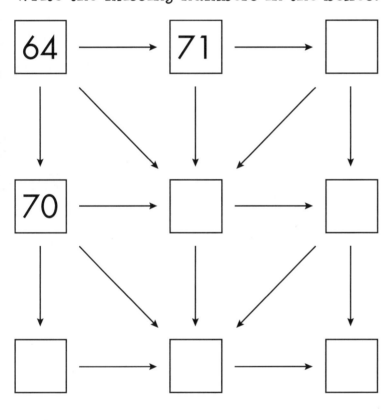

What addition could be written next to diagonal arrows like this (↘)? Write it in the diagram.

Why does this addition work?

_____

_____

What calculation would be written next to arrows like this (↙)? Write it in the diagram.

Teacher's notes

Suggested objective: *Identify and use patterns, relationships and properties of numbers.*

This activity will provide practice in addition as well as in logical thinking. Can the pupils identify the relationship that each arrow represents? Some pupils will complete the puzzle very quickly, although many make mistakes in identifying what should be written next to the diagonal arrows. When you are confident that the pupils have completed the puzzle, extend the activity by asking them how many number sequences can be found on the diagram then to continue each of these sequences to beyond 100.

Name _____ Date _____

Can you find and follow the patterns?

Look at the diagram.

For every horizontal arrow (→) you must always add the same number. Find the number.

For every vertical arrow (↓) you must always add the same number. Find the number.

Write the missing numbers in the boxes.

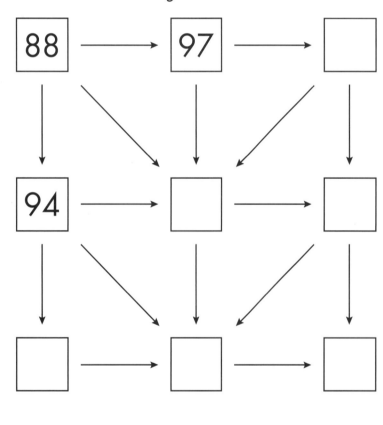

What addition could be written next to diagonal arrows like this (↘)? Write it in the diagram.

Why does this addition work?

_____

_____

What calculation would be written next to arrows like this (↗)? Write it in the diagram.

Teacher's notes

Suggested objective: *Identify and use patterns, relationships and properties of numbers.*

This activity will provide practice in addition as well as in logical thinking. Can the pupils identify the relationship that each arrow represents? Some pupils will complete the puzzle very quickly, although many make mistakes in identifying what should be written next to the diagonal arrows. When you are confident that the pupils have completed the puzzle, extend the activity by asking them how many number sequences can be found on the diagram then to continue each of these sequences to beyond 200.

Andrew Brodie: Maths Puzzles and Games 9–11 © A&C Black 2011

Name _____ *Date* _____

Can you follow the patterns?

Look at the diagram.

For every horizontal arrow (→) you must always subtract 7.

For every vertical arrow (↓) you must always subtract 12.

Write the missing numbers in the boxes.

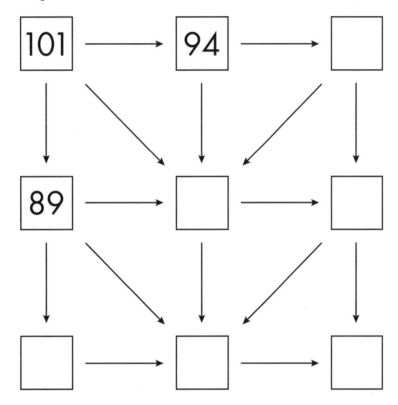

What subtraction could be written next to diagonal arrows like this (↘)? Write it in the diagram.

What subtraction would be written next to arrows like this (↙)? Write it in the diagram.

Teacher's notes

Suggested objective: *Identify and use patterns, relationships and properties of numbers.*

This activity will provide practice in subtraction as well as in logical thinking. Can the pupils identify the relationship that each arrow represents? Some pupils will complete the puzzle very quickly, although many make mistakes in identifying what should be written next to the diagonal arrows. When you are confident that the pupils have completed the puzzle, extend the activity by asking them how many number sequences can be found on the diagram then to continue each of these sequences to beyond 0.

Name _____ Date _____

Can you follow the patterns?

Look at the diagram.

For every horizontal arrow (→)
you must always subtract 14.

For every vertical arrow you (↓)
must always subtract 16.

Write the missing numbers in the boxes.

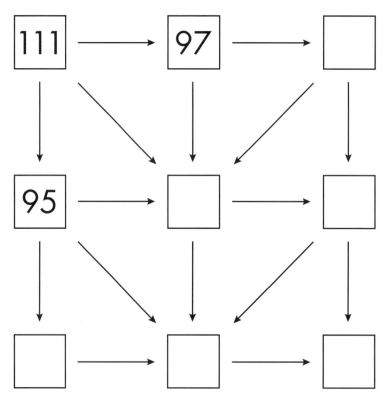

What subtraction could be
written next to diagonal arrows
like this (↘)? Write it in the
diagram.

What subtraction would be
written next to arrows like this
(↙)? Write it in the diagram.

Teacher's notes

Suggested objective: *Identify and use patterns, relationships and properties of numbers.*

This activity will provide practice in subtraction as well as in logical thinking. Can the pupils identify the relationship that each arrow represents? Some pupils will complete the puzzle very quickly, although many make mistakes in identifying what should be written next to the diagonal arrows. When you are confident that the pupils have completed the puzzle, extend the activity by asking them how many number sequences can be found on the diagram then to continue each of these sequences to beyond 0.

Name _____ Date _____

Can you find and follow the patterns?

Look at the diagram.

For every horizontal arrow (→) you must always subtract the same number. Find the number.

For every vertical arrow (↓) you must always subtract the same number. Find the number.

Write the missing numbers in the boxes.

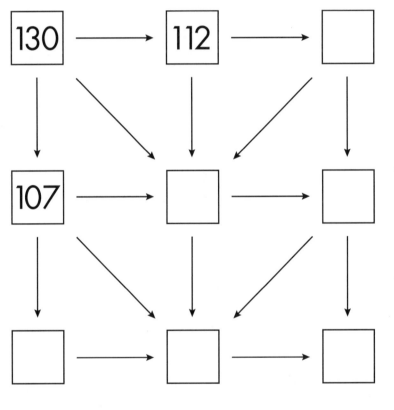

What subtraction could be written next to diagonal arrows like this (↘)? Write it in the diagram.

Why does this subtraction work?

_____

_____

What calculation would be written next to arrows like this (↙)?

Teacher's notes

Suggested objective: *Identify and use patterns, relationships and properties of numbers.*

This activity will provide practice in subtraction as well as in logical thinking. Can the pupils identify the relationship that each arrow represents? Some pupils will complete the puzzle very quickly, although many make mistakes in identifying what should be written next to the diagonal arrows. When you are confident that the pupils have completed the puzzle, extend the activity by asking them how many number sequences can be found on the diagram then to continue each of these sequences to beyond 0.

Name _____ Date _____

Can you find and follow the patterns?

Look at the diagram.

For every horizontal arrow (→) you must always subtract the same number. Find the number.

For every vertical arrow (↓) you must always subtract the same number. Find the number.

Write the missing numbers in the boxes.

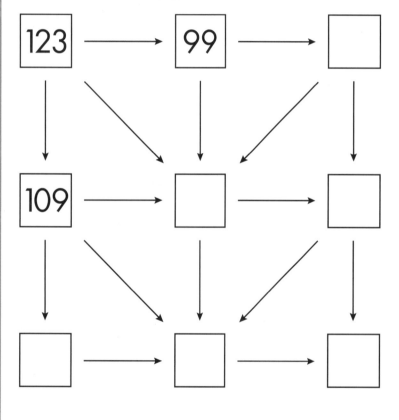

What subtraction could be written next to diagonal arrows like this (↘)? Write it in the diagram.

Why does this subtraction work?

_____

_____

What calculation would be written next to arrows like this (↙)?

Teacher's notes

Suggested objective: *Identify and use patterns, relationships and properties of numbers.*

This activity will provide practice in subtraction as well as in logical thinking. Can the pupils identify the relationship that each arrow represents? Are they surprised by the calculation needed for the second diagonal arrow? Some pupils will complete the puzzle very quickly, although many make mistakes in identifying what should be written next to the diagonal arrows. When you are confident that the pupils have completed the puzzle, extend the activity by asking them how many number sequences can be found on the diagram then to continue each of these sequences to beyond 0.

Name _____ *Date* _____

Can you play thousands bingo?

2500		1648		7982
9006	3215		8400	1792
	4029	5000		

2500		1648	3942	
	7300	4107		5252
6215		8079		9000

		3942		7300
4250	8999		5706	
9500		1014	2050	6000

4250	8999		3004	
	5917	6098	1140	2345
		7350		4000

Teacher's notes

Suggested objective: *Recognise four-digit whole numbers.*

These bingo cards should be used in conjunction with the number cards on sheet 22. Pupils match the numbers called to the numbers on their bingo card. Pupils should also be supplied with some blank cards or counters to cover their numbers as they are called out. 'Bingo' is called out by a pupil when he makes a line.

Name _____ Date _____

Can you play thousands bingo?

2500	1648	7982	9006	3215
8400	1792	4029	5000	3942
7300	4107	5252	6215	8079
9000	4250	8999	5706	9500
1014	2050	6000	3004	5917
6098	1140	2345	7350	4000

Teacher's notes

Suggested objective: *Recognise four-digit whole numbers.*

These number cards should be used in conjunction with the bingo cards on sheet 21. Pupils should also be supplied with some blank cards or counters to cover their numbers as they are called out. The caller will call out each number at random for pupils to match to a number on their bingo card.

Andrew Brodie: Maths Puzzles and Games 9–11 © A&C Black 2011

Name _____ Date _____

Can you follow the patterns?

Look at the diagram.

For every horizontal arrow (→) you must always multiply by 4.

For every vertical arrow (↓) you must always multiply by 5.

Write the missing numbers in the boxes.

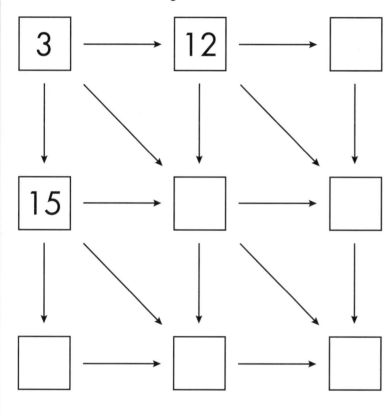

What multiplication could be written next to the diagonal arrow (↘)? Write it in the diagram.

Why does this number work?

_____

_____

Teacher's notes

Suggested objective: *Identify and use patterns, relationships and properties of numbers.*

This activity will provide practice in multiplication and division as well as in logical thinking. This puzzle requires advanced skills in multiplication. Can the pupils identify the relationship that the diagonal arrow represents? Some pupils will complete the puzzle quite quickly, although many make mistakes in identifying what should be written next to the diagonal arrows. When you are confident that the pupils have completed the puzzle, extend the activity by asking them how many number sequences can be found on the diagram then to continue each of these sequences to beyond 200.

Name _____ *Date* _____

Can you follow the patterns?

Look at the diagram.

For every horizontal arrow (→) you must always multiply by 6.

For every vertical arrow (↓) you must always multiply by 4.

Write the missing numbers in the boxes.

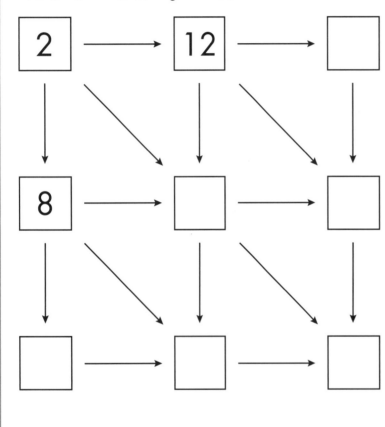

What multiplication could be written next to the diagonal arrow (↘)? Write it in the diagram.

Why does this number work?

_____

_____

Teacher's notes

Suggested objective: *Identify and use patterns, relationships and properties of numbers.*

This activity will provide practice in multiplication and division as well as in logical thinking. This puzzle requires advanced skills in multiplication. Can the pupils identify the relationship that the diagonal arrow represents? Some pupils will complete the puzzle quite quickly, although many make mistakes in identifying what should be written next to the diagonal arrows. When you are confident that the pupils have completed the puzzle, extend the activity by asking them how many number sequences can be found on the diagram then to continue each of these sequences to beyond 200.

Name _____ *Date* _____

Can you follow the patterns?

Look at the diagram.

For every horizontal arrow (→) you must always multiply by 7.

For every vertical arrow (↓) you must always multiply by 4.

Write the missing numbers in the boxes.

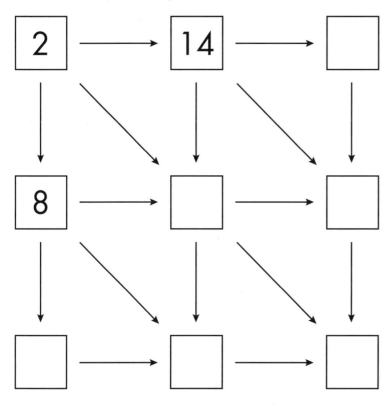

What multiplication could be written next to the diagonal arrow (↘)? Write it in the diagram.

Why does this number work?

_____

_____

Teacher's notes

Suggested objective: *Identify and use patterns, relationships and properties of numbers.*

This activity will provide practice in multiplication and division as well as in logical thinking. This puzzle requires advanced skills in multiplication. Can the pupils identify the relationship that the diagonal arrow represents? Some pupils will complete the puzzle quite quickly, although many make mistakes in identifying what should be written next to the diagonal arrows. When you are confident that the pupils have completed the puzzle, extend the activity by asking them how many number sequences can be found on the diagram then to continue each of these sequences to beyond 200.

Name _____ Date _____

Can you find and follow the patterns?

Look at the diagram.

For every horizontal arrow (→) you must always multiply by the same number.

For every vertical arrow (↓) you must always multiply by the same number.

Write the missing numbers in the boxes.

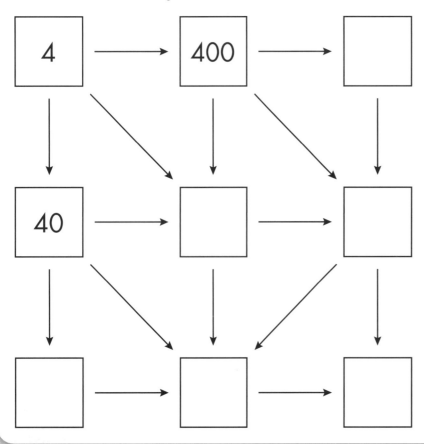

What multiplication could be written next to each arrow (→↓↘)? Write it in the diagram.

What division would be written next to arrows like this (↗)? Write it in the diagram.

Teacher's notes

Suggested objective: *Identify and use patterns, relationships and properties of numbers.*

This activity will provide practice in multiplication and division as well as in logical thinking. This puzzle requires advanced skills in multiplication. Can the pupils identify the relationship that each arrow represents? Some pupils will complete the puzzle quite quickly, although many make mistakes in identifying what should be written next to the diagonal arrows. When you are confident that the pupils have completed the puzzle, extend the activity by asking them how many number sequences can be found on the diagram then to continue each of these sequences to contain at least six numbers.

Andrew Brodie: Maths Puzzles and Games 9–11 © A&C Black 2011

Name _____ Date _____

Can you play decimals bingo?

0.9		0.37		1.34
	6.75	9.5		4.25
23.48	0.96		14.4	

0.9	0.37		5.48	
	2.59	8.2	7.07	36.52
	0.46			17.8

	5.48			2.59
0.6	0.72		7.3	8.14
47.63		0.81		19.9

0.6	0.72		3.07	
5.43		6.2		9.29
72.72	0.75		16.2	

Teacher's notes

Suggested objective: *Recognise decimal numbers.*

These bingo cards should be used in conjunction with the number cards on sheet 28. Pupils match the numbers called to the numbers on their bingo card. Pupils should also be supplied with some blank cards or counters to cover their numbers as they are called out. 'Bingo' is called out by a pupil when he makes a line.

Name _____ *Date* _____

Can you play decimals bingo?

0.9	0.37	1.34	6.75	9.5
4.25	23.48	0.96	14.4	5.48
2.59	8.2	7.07	36.52	0.46
17.8	0.6	0.72	7.3	8.14
47.63	0.81	19.9	3.07	5.43
6.2	9.29	72.72	0.75	16.2

Teacher's notes

Suggested objective: *Recognise decimal numbers.*

These number cards should be used in conjunction with the bingo cards on sheet 27. Pupils should also be supplied with some blank cards or counters to cover their numbers as they are called out. The caller will call out each number at random for pupils to match to a number on their bingo card.

Andrew Brodie: Maths Puzzles and Games 9–11 © A&C Black 2011

Name _____ *Date* _____

Can you find and follow the patterns?

Look at the diagram.

For every horizontal arrow (→) you must always multiply by the same number.

For every vertical arrow (↓) you must always multiply by the same number.

Write the missing numbers in the boxes.

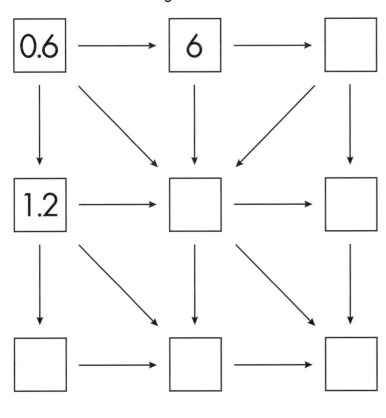

What multiplication could be written next to each arrow (→ ↓ ↘)? Write it in the diagram.

What division would be written next to arrows like this (↗)? Write it in the diagram.

Name _____ Date _____

Can you find and follow the patterns?

Look at the diagram.

For every horizontal arrow (→) you must always multiply by the same number.

For every vertical arrow (↓) you must always multiply by the same number.

Write the missing numbers in the boxes.

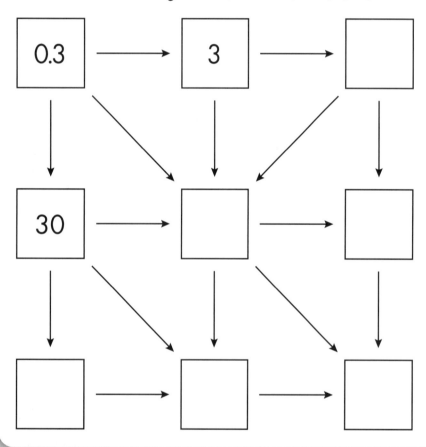

What multiplication could be written next to each arrow (→↓↘)? Write it in the diagram.

What multiplication would be written next to arrows like this (↗)? Write it in the diagram.

Teacher's notes

Suggested objective: *Identify and use patterns, relationships and properties of numbers.*

This activity will provide practice in multiplication and division as well as in logical thinking. This puzzle requires advanced skills in multiplication. Can the pupils identify the relationship that each arrow represents? Some pupils will complete the puzzle quite quickly, although many make mistakes in identifying what should be written next to the diagonal arrows. When you are confident that the pupils have completed the puzzle, extend the activity by asking them how many number sequences can be found on the diagram then to continue each of these sequences to contain at least six numbers.

Andrew Brodie: Maths Puzzles and Games 9–11 © A&C Black 2011

Name _____ *Date* _____

Can you play number variety bingo?

27000	614		47	
3204		36423		17500
		850	9024	75420

27000	614		59	4659
38500	14306	618		
		8245		67250

	59	4659		45000
924	42137		18204	
872			7114	86319

45000		924		76
	2960	62017		12416
745	6745		73864	

Teacher's notes

Suggested objective: *Recognise a variety of whole numbers.*

These bingo cards should be used in conjunction with the number cards on sheet 32. Pupils match the numbers called to the numbers on their bingo card. Pupils should also be supplied with some blank cards or counters to cover their numbers as they are called out. 'Bingo' is called out by a pupil when he makes a line.

Name _____ Date _____

Can you play number variety bingo?

27000	614	47	3204	36423
17500	850	9024	75420	59
4659	38500	14306	618	8245
67250	45000	924	42137	18204
872	7114	86319	76	2960
62017	12416	745	6745	73864

Teacher's notes

Suggested objective: *Recognise a variety of whole numbers.*

These number cards should be used in conjunction with the bingo cards on sheet 31. Pupils should also be supplied with some blank cards or counters to cover their numbers as they are called out. The caller will call out each number at random for pupils to match to a number on their bingo card.

Andrew Brodie: Maths Puzzles and Games 9–11 © A&C Black 2011

Name _____ *Date* _____

Can you find all the triangles?

How many triangles can you see in this picture?

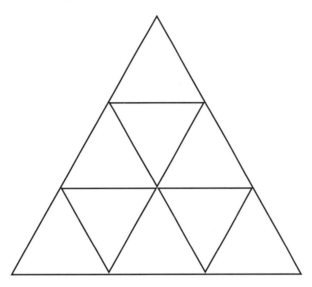

Here are some extra copies of the picture so that you can find all the triangles.

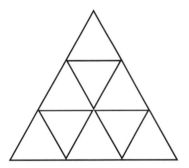   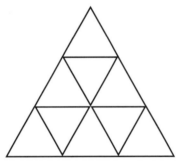   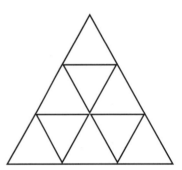

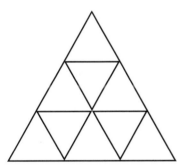   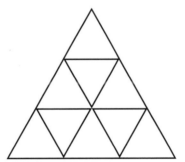

Teacher's notes

Suggested objective: *Identify and use properties of triangles.*

The children may be surprised by the number of triangles that can be found in the diagram.

Andrew Brodie: Maths Puzzles and Games 9–11 © A&C Black 2011

Name _____ *Date* _____

Can you find all the rhombuses?

How many rhombuses can you see
in this picture?

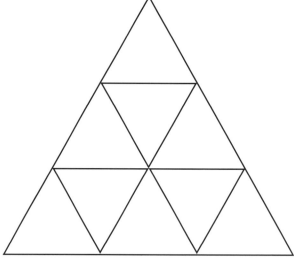

Here are some extra copies of the picture so that you can find all
the rhombuses.

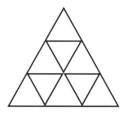 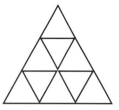  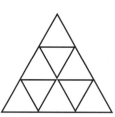 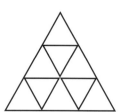

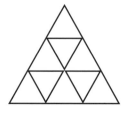 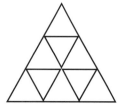 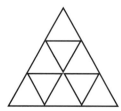 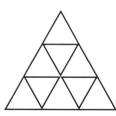 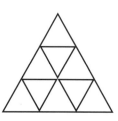

Teacher's notes

Suggested objective: *Identify and use properties of rhombuses.*

The children need to understand the properties of rhombuses to be able to find all of those that appear in
this diagram.

Andrew Brodie: Maths Puzzles and Games 9–11 © A&C Black 2011

Name _____ *Date* _____

Can you find all the trapeziums?

How many trapeziums can you see
in this picture?

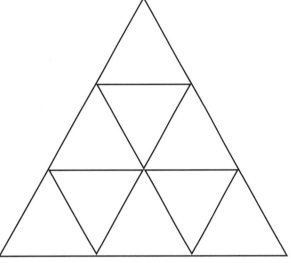

Here are some extra copies of the picture so that
you can find all the trapeziums.

Teacher's notes

Suggested objective: *Identify and use properties of trapeziums.*

The children need to understand the properties of trapeziums to be able to find all of those that appear in
this diagram.

Andrew Brodie: Maths Puzzles and Games 9–11 © A&C Black 2011

Name _____ *Date* _____

Can you complete the magic squares?

In a magic square the numbers in each row (→), each column (↓) and each diagonal (↘) all add up to the same value, called the 'magic number'.

What is the magic number in the magic square below? [   ]

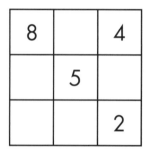

Now find all the missing numbers in the magic square. Every number must be different.

What is the magic number in the magic square below? [   ]

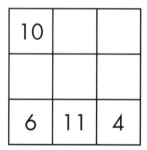

Now find all the missing numbers in the magic square. Every number must be different.

Teacher's notes

Suggested objective: *Use knowledge of number facts and inverse operations to estimate and check calculations.*

Are the pupils aware that they can find the 'magic number' by adding together the numbers where there is a complete set of three? Do they understand that they need to find the missing numbers systematically by identifying sets of three where only one number is missing?

Name _____ *Date* _____

Can you complete the magic squares?

In a magic square the numbers in each row (→), each column (↓) and each diagonal (↘) all add up to the same value, called the 'magic number'.

What is the magic number in the magic square below? [   ]

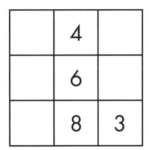

	4	
	6	
	8	3

Now find all the missing numbers in the magic square. Every number must be different.

What is the magic number in the magic square below? [   ]

	1	
	5	
	9	2

Now find all the missing numbers in the magic square. Every number must be different.

Teacher's notes

Suggested objective: *Use knowledge of number facts and inverse operations to estimate and check calculations.*

Are the pupils aware that they can find the 'magic number' by adding together the numbers where there is a complete set of three? Do they understand that they need to find the missing numbers systematically by identifying sets of three where only one number is missing?

Name _____ *Date* _____

Can you complete the magic squares?

In a magic square the numbers in each row (→), each column (↓) and each diagonal (↘) all add up to the same value, called the 'magic number'.

What is the magic number in the magic square below?

	13	
	15	
16	17	

Now find all the missing numbers in the magic square. Every number must be different.

What is the magic number in the magic square below?

	14	19
	18	
17		

Now find all the missing numbers in the magic square. Every number must be different.

Teacher's notes

Suggested objective: *Use knowledge of number facts and inverse operations to estimate and check calculations.*

Are the pupils aware that they can find the 'magic number' by adding together the numbers where there is a complete set of three? Do they understand that they need to find the missing numbers systematically by identifying sets of three where only one number is missing?

Andrew Brodie: Maths Puzzles and Games 9–11 © A&C Black 2011

Name _____ *Date* _____

Can you complete the magic squares?

In a magic square the numbers in each row (→), each column (↓) and each diagonal (↘) all add up to the same value, called the 'magic number'.

What is the magic number in the magic square below? ☐

14		
	15	
18		16

Now find all the missing numbers in the magic square. Every number must be different.

What is the magic number in the magic square below? ☐

	15	20
	19	
18		

Now find all the missing numbers in the magic square. Every number must be different.

Teacher's notes

Suggested objective: *Use knowledge of number facts and inverse operations to estimate and check calculations.*

Are the pupils aware that they can find the 'magic number' by adding together the numbers where there is a complete set of three? Do they understand that they need to find the missing numbers systematically by identifying sets of three where only one number is missing?

Name _____   Date _____

Can you complete the magic squares?

In a magic square the numbers in each row (→), each column (↓) and each diagonal (↘) all add up to the same value, called the 'magic number'.

What is the magic number in the magic square below? [   ]

	1.1	
	0.7	
1	0.3	

Now find all the missing numbers in the magic square. Every number must be different.

What is the magic number in the magic square below? [   ]

0.6	1.1	1
	0.9	

Now find all the missing numbers in the magic square. Every number must be different.

Teacher's notes

Suggested objective: *Use knowledge of number facts and inverse operations to estimate and check calculations when finding sums and differences of decimals.*

Are the pupils aware that they can find the 'magic number' by adding together the numbers where there is a complete set of three? Do they understand that they need to find the missing numbers systematically by identifying sets of three where only one number is missing?

Andrew Brodie: Maths Puzzles and Games 9–11 © A&C Black 2011

Name _____ Date _____

Can you complete the magic squares?

In a magic square the numbers in each row (→), each column (↓) and each diagonal (↘) all add up to the same value, called the 'magic number'.

What is the magic number in the magic square below? [   ]

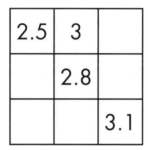

2.5	3	
	2.8	
		3.1

Now find all the missing numbers in the magic square. Every number must be different.

What is the magic number in the magic square below? [   ]

0.3		
1.1	0.6	0.1

Now find all the missing numbers in the magic square. Every number must be different.

Teacher's notes

Suggested objective: *Use knowledge of number facts and inverse operations to estimate and check calculations when finding sums and differences of decimals.*

Are the pupils aware that they can find the 'magic number' by adding together the numbers where there is a complete set of three? Do they understand that they need to find the missing numbers systematically by identifying sets of three where only one number is missing?

Name _____ Date _____

Can you complete the magic squares?

In a magic square the numbers in each row (→), each column (↓) and each diagonal (↘) all add up to the same value, called the 'magic number'.

What is the magic number in the magic square below? [ ]

	1.1	
	0.8	
	0.5	1.2

Now find all the missing numbers in the magic square. Every number must be different.

What is the magic number in the magic square below? [ ]

9.3		
10.5		9.1
9.6		

Now find all the missing numbers in the magic square. Every number must be different.

Teacher's notes

Suggested objective: *Use knowledge of number facts and inverse operations to estimate and check calculations when finding sums and differences of decimals.*

Are the pupils aware that they can find the 'magic number' by adding together the numbers where there is a complete set of three? Do they understand that they need to find the missing numbers systematically by identifying sets of three where only one number is missing?

Name _____   *Date* _____

Can you complete the magic square?

In a magic square the numbers in each row (→), each column (↓) and each diagonal (↘) all add up to the same value, called the 'magic number'.

What is the magic number in the magic square below? [   ]

	11	7	4
5	6	10	
	9		
	12		3

Now find all the missing numbers in the magic square. Every number must be different.

Teacher's notes

Suggested objective: *Use knowledge of number facts and inverse operations to estimate and check calculations.*

Are the pupils aware that they can find the 'magic number' by adding together the numbers where there is a complete set of four? Do they understand that they need to find the missing numbers systematically by identifying sets of four where only one number is missing?

Name _____ *Date* _____

Can you complete the magic square?

In a magic square the numbers in each row (→), each column (↓) and each diagonal (↘) all add up to the same value, called the 'magic number'.

What is the magic number in the magic square below? [   ]

		6	1
0		11	12
	4		
14	9		2

Now find all the missing numbers in the magic square. Every number must be different.

Teacher's notes

Suggested objective: *Use knowledge of number facts and inverse operations to estimate and check calculations.*

Are the pupils aware that they can find the 'magic number' by adding together the numbers where there is a complete set of four? Do they understand that they need to find the missing numbers systematically by identifying sets of four where only one number is missing?

Andrew Brodie: Maths Puzzles and Games 9–11 © A&C Black 2011

Name _____ *Date* _____

Can you complete the magic square?

In a magic square the numbers in each row (→), each column (↓) and each diagonal (↘) all add up to the same value, called the 'magic number'.

What is the magic number in the magic square below? [   ]

1.4	0.9	0.5	0.2
0.3			
	0.7	1.1	
1.3			0.1

Now find all the missing numbers in the magic square. Every number must be different.

Teacher's notes

Suggested objective: *Use knowledge of number facts and inverse operations to estimate and check calculations when finding sums and differences of decimals.*

Are the pupils aware that they can find the 'magic number' by adding together the numbers where there is a complete set of four? Do they understand that they need to find the missing numbers systematically by identifying sets of four where only one number is missing?

Name _____ Date _____

Can you complete the magic square?

In a magic square the numbers in each row (→), each column (↓) and each diagonal (↘) all add up to the same value, called the 'magic number'.

What is the magic number in the magic square below? [   ]

1.9		1	0.7
	0.9	1.3	
		1.6	1.7
1.8		1.1	

Now find all the missing numbers in the magic square. Every number must be different.

Teacher's notes

Suggested objective: *Use knowledge of number facts and inverse operations to estimate and check calculations when finding sums and differences of decimals.*

Are the pupils aware that they can find the 'magic number' by adding together the numbers where there is a complete set of four? Do they understand that they need to find the missing numbers systematically by identifying sets of four where only one number is missing?

Name _____ *Date* _____

How quickly can you complete each number train?

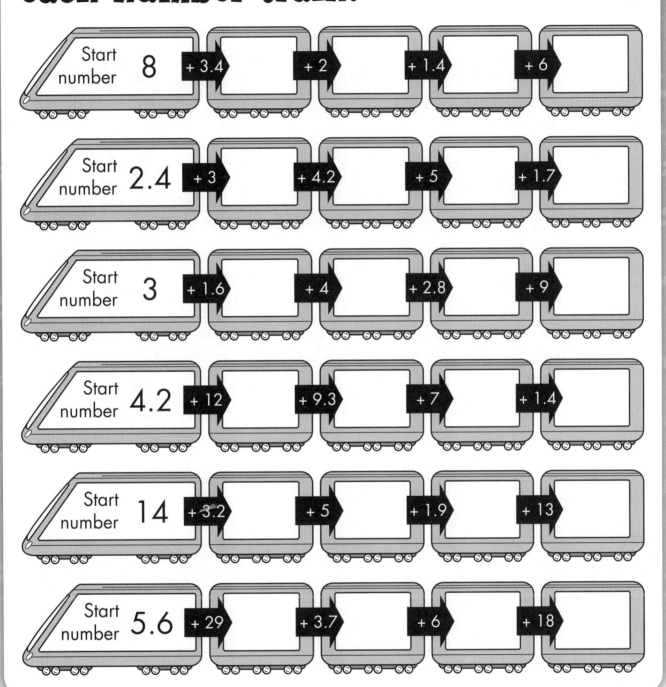

Start number **8** → +3.4 → ☐ → +2 → ☐ → +1.4 → ☐ → +6 → ☐

Start number **2.4** → +3 → ☐ → +4.2 → ☐ → +5 → ☐ → +1.7 → ☐

Start number **3** → +1.6 → ☐ → +4 → ☐ → +2.8 → ☐ → +9 → ☐

Start number **4.2** → +12 → ☐ → +9.3 → ☐ → +7 → ☐ → +1.4 → ☐

Start number **14** → +3.2 → ☐ → +5 → ☐ → +1.9 → ☐ → +13 → ☐

Start number **5.6** → +29 → ☐ → +3.7 → ☐ → +6 → ☐ → +18 → ☐

Teacher's notes

Suggested objective: *Derive sums of decimals using knowledge of place value and addition.*

The children could use the class clock to time themselves completing each train.

Name _____ Date _____

How quickly can you complete each number train?

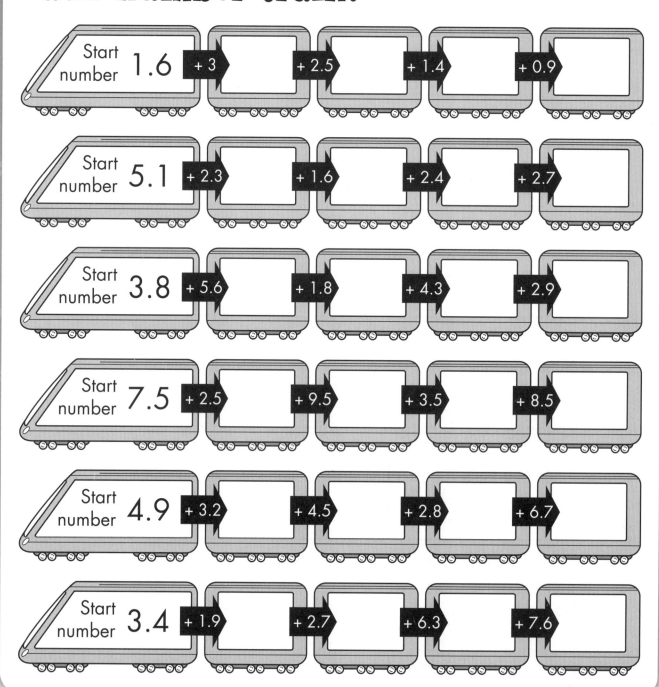

Start number 1.6 → +3 → ☐ → +2.5 → ☐ → +1.4 → ☐ → +0.9 → ☐

Start number 5.1 → +2.3 → ☐ → +1.6 → ☐ → +2.4 → ☐ → +2.7 → ☐

Start number 3.8 → +5.6 → ☐ → +1.8 → ☐ → +4.3 → ☐ → +2.9 → ☐

Start number 7.5 → +2.5 → ☐ → +9.5 → ☐ → +3.5 → ☐ → +8.5 → ☐

Start number 4.9 → +3.2 → ☐ → +4.5 → ☐ → +2.8 → ☐ → +6.7 → ☐

Start number 3.4 → +1.9 → ☐ → +2.7 → ☐ → +6.3 → ☐ → +7.6 → ☐

Teacher's notes

Suggested objective: *Derive sums of decimals using knowledge of place value and addition.*

The children could use the class clock to time themselves completing each train.

Andrew Brodie: Maths Puzzles and Games 9–11 © A&C Black 2011

Name _____   Date _____

How quickly can you complete each number train?

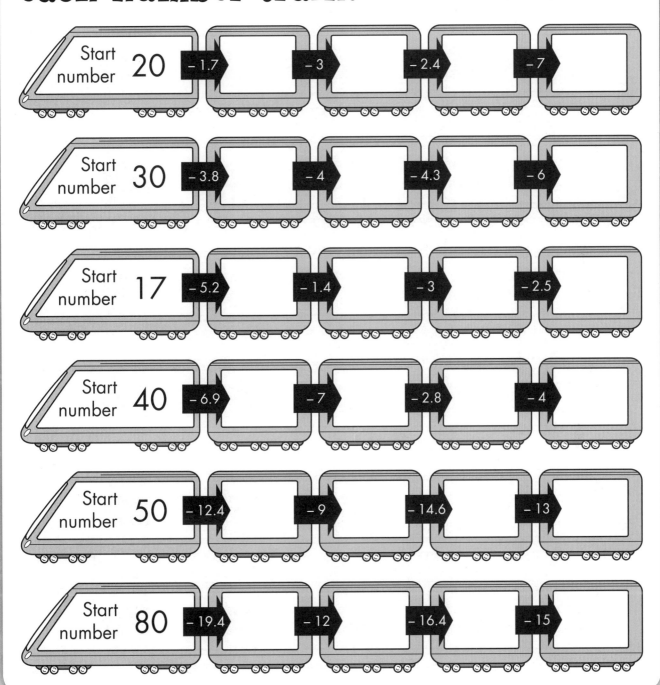

Start number **20** | −1.7 | | −3 | | −2.4 | | −7 |

Start number **30** | −3.8 | | −4 | | −4.3 | | −6 |

Start number **17** | −5.2 | | −1.4 | | −3 | | −2.5 |

Start number **40** | −6.9 | | −7 | | −2.8 | | −4 |

Start number **50** | −12.4 | | −9 | | −14.6 | | −13 |

Start number **80** | −19.4 | | −12 | | −16.4 | | −15 |

Teacher's notes

Suggested objective: *Derive differences of decimals using knowledge of place value and subtraction.*

The children could use the class clock to time themselves completing each train.

Name _____ Date _____

How quickly can you complete each number train?

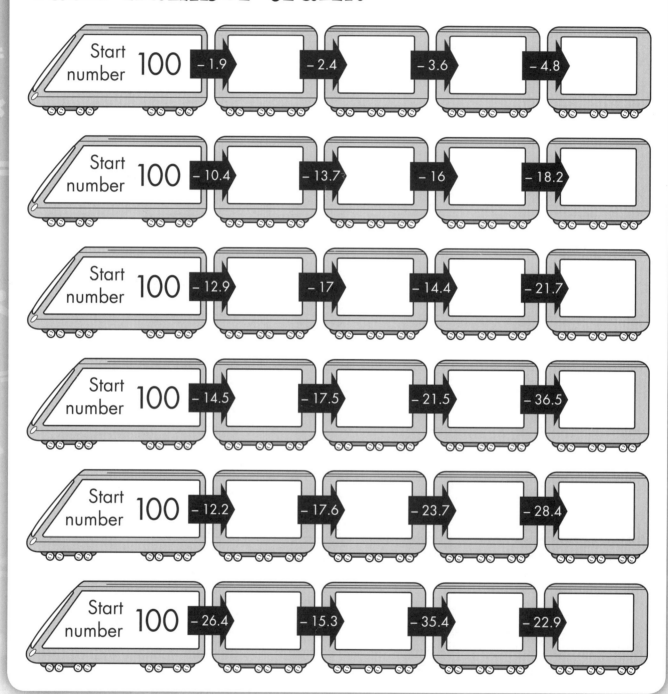

Start number 100 −1.9 □ −2.4 □ −3.6 □ −4.8 □

Start number 100 −10.4 □ −13.7 □ −16 □ −18.2 □

Start number 100 −12.9 □ −17 □ −14.4 □ −21.7 □

Start number 100 −14.5 □ −17.5 □ −21.5 □ −36.5 □

Start number 100 −12.2 □ −17.6 □ −23.7 □ −28.4 □

Start number 100 −26.4 □ −15.3 □ −35.4 □ −22.9 □

Teacher's notes

Suggested objective: *Derive differences of decimals using knowledge of place value and subtraction.*

The children could use the class clock to time themselves completing each train.

Name _____ *Date* _____

How quickly can you complete each number train?

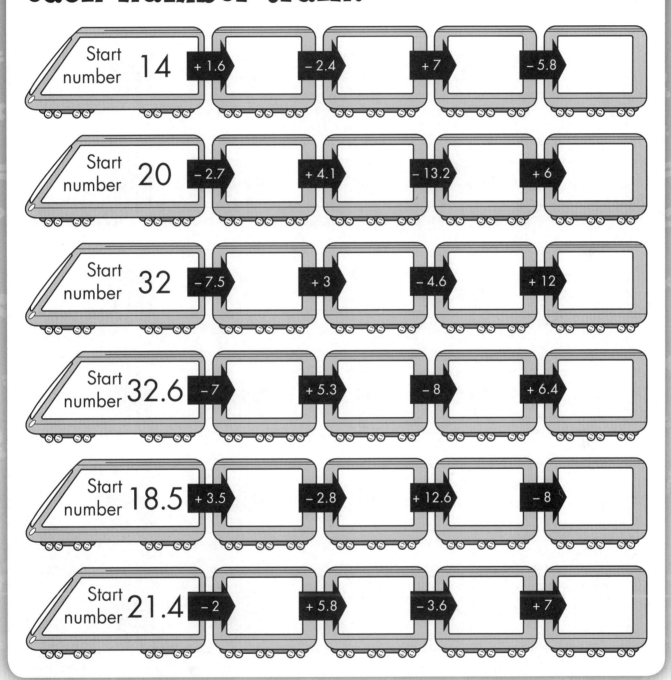

Start number **14** → + 1.6 → ☐ → − 2.4 → ☐ → + 7 → ☐ → − 5.8 → ☐

Start number **20** → − 2.7 → ☐ → + 4.1 → ☐ → − 13.2 → ☐ → + 6 → ☐

Start number **32** → − 7.5 → ☐ → + 3 → ☐ → − 4.6 → ☐ → + 12 → ☐

Start number **32.6** → − 7 → ☐ → + 5.3 → ☐ → − 8 → ☐ → + 6.4 → ☐

Start number **18.5** → + 3.5 → ☐ → − 2.8 → ☐ → + 12.6 → ☐ → − 8 → ☐

Start number **21.4** → − 2 → ☐ → + 5.8 → ☐ → − 3.6 → ☐ → + 7 → ☐

Teacher's notes

Suggested objective: *Derive sums and differences of decimals using knowledge of place value and addition and subtraction.*

The children could use the class clock to time themselves completing each train.

Name _____ Date _____

How quickly can you complete each number train?

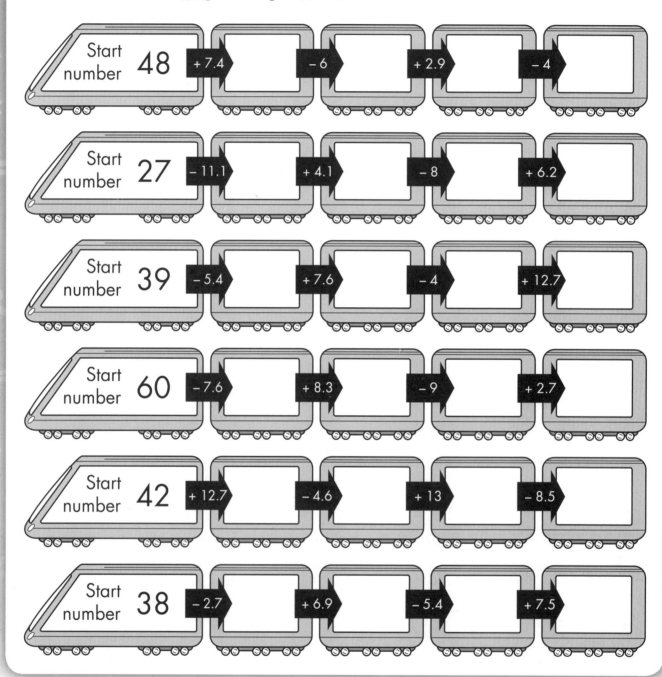

Start number **48** | +7.4 | | −6 | | +2.9 | | −4 |

Start number **27** | −11.1 | | +4.1 | | −8 | | +6.2 |

Start number **39** | −5.4 | | +7.6 | | −4 | | +12.7 |

Start number **60** | −7.6 | | +8.3 | | −9 | | +2.7 |

Start number **42** | +12.7 | | −4.6 | | +13 | | −8.5 |

Start number **38** | −2.7 | | +6.9 | | −5.4 | | +7.5 |

Teacher's notes

Suggested objective: *Derive sums and differences of decimals using knowledge of place value and addition and subtraction.*

The children could use the class clock to time themselves completing each train.

Name _____ *Date* _____

Can you find the patterns on a hundred square?

1	2	3	4	5	6	7	8	9	10
11	12	13	14	15	16	17	18	19	20
21	22	23	24	25	26	27	28	29	30
31	32	33	34	35	36	37	38	39	40
41	42	43	44	45	46	47	48	49	50
51	52	53	54	55	56	57	58	59	60
61	62	63	64	65	66	67	68	69	70
71	72	73	74	75	76	77	78	79	80
81	82	83	84	85	86	87	88	89	90
91	92	93	94	95	96	97	98	99	100

Teacher's notes

Suggested objective: *Explore patterns, properties and relationships.*

Explore patterns, properties and relationships.

Name _____ *Date* _____

Can you find the patterns on a hundred square?

Here is part of a
hundred square.

33	34	35
43	44	45
53	54	55

Look for patterns.

Try adding all the horizontals.

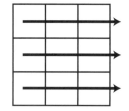

Try adding all the verticals.

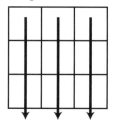

Try adding this diagonal.

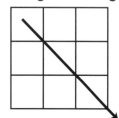

Try adding this diagonal.

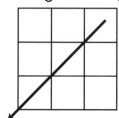

Try adding the sums of the horizontals. Try adding the sums of
the verticals.

Try multiplying the centre number by 9 (the number of numbers).

Teacher's notes

Suggested objective: *Explore patterns, properties and relationships.*

Encourage the pupils to experiment with adding and with multiplying. How many relationships can they find?

Andrew Brodie: Maths Puzzles and Games 9–11 © A&C Black 2011

Name _____ Date _____

Can you find the patterns on a hundred square?

Here is part of a hundred square.

67	68	69
77	78	79
87	88	89

Look for patterns.

Try adding all the horizontals.

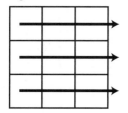

Try adding all the verticals.

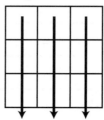

Try adding this diagonal.

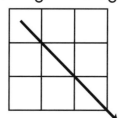

Try adding this diagonal.

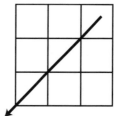

Try adding the sums of the horizontals. Try adding the sums of the verticals.

Try multiplying the centre number by 9 (the number of numbers).

Teacher's notes

Suggested objective: *Explore patterns, properties and relationships.*

Encourage the pupils to experiment with adding and with multiplying. How many relationships can they find? Do they find similar relationships to those they found on the previous sheet?

Name _____ Date _____

Can you find the patterns on a hundred square?

Choose a three by three section of a hundred square.

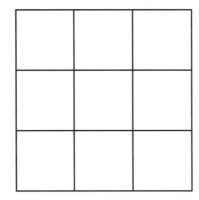

Look for patterns.

Try adding all the horizontals.

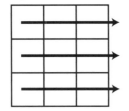

Try adding all the verticals.

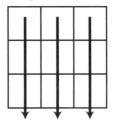

Try adding this diagonal.

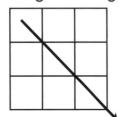

Try adding this diagonal.

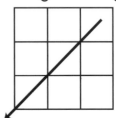

Try adding the sums of the horizontals. Try adding the sums of the verticals.

Try multiplying the centre number by 9 (the number of numbers).

Teacher's notes

Suggested objective: *Explore patterns, properties and relationships.*

Encourage the pupils to experiment with adding and with multiplying. How many relationships can they find? Do they find similar relationships to those they found on the previous sheets?

Name _____ *Date* _____

Can you find the patterns on a hundred square?

Here is part of a hundred square.

16	17	18	19
26	27	28	29
36	37	38	39
46	47	48	49

Look for patterns.

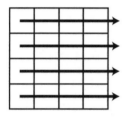

Try adding all the horizontals.

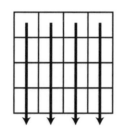

Try adding all the verticals.

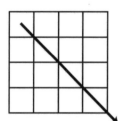

Try adding this diagonal.

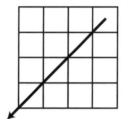

Try adding this diagonal.

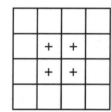

Try adding the four centre numbers, then multiplying the answer by four.

Try adding the sums of the horizontals and finding the mean average.

Try adding the sums of the verticals and finding the mean average.

Teacher's notes

Suggested objective: *Explore patterns, properties and relationships.*

Encourage the pupils to experiment with adding and with multiplying. How many relationships can they find?

Name _____ *Date* _____

Can you find the patterns on a hundred square?

Choose a four by four section of a hundred square.

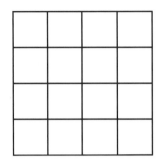

Look for patterns.

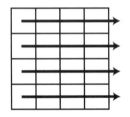

Try adding all the horizontals.

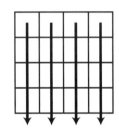

Try adding all the verticals.

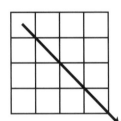

Try adding this diagonal.

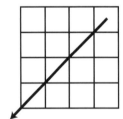

Try adding this diagonal.

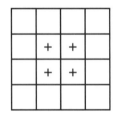

Try adding the four centre numbers, then multiplying the answer by four.

Try adding the sums of the horizontals and finding the mean average.

Try adding the sums of the verticals and finding the mean average.

Teacher's notes

Suggested objective: *Explore patterns, properties and relationships.*

Encourage the pupils to experiment with adding and with multiplying. How many relationships can they find? Do they find similar relationships to those they found on the previous sheet?

Andrew Brodie: Maths Puzzles and Games 9–11 © A&C Black 2011

Name _____ Date _____

Can you find the patterns on a hundred square?

Here is part of a hundred square.

36	37	38	39	40
46	47	48	49	50
56	57	58	59	60
66	67	68	69	70
76	77	78	79	80

Look for patterns.

Try adding all the horizontals.

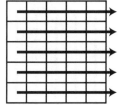

Try adding all the verticals.

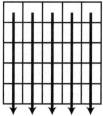

Try adding this diagonal.

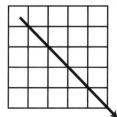

Try adding this diagonal.

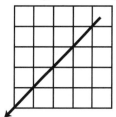

Try adding the sums of the horizontals. Try adding the sums of the verticals.

Try multiplying the centre number by 25 (the number of numbers).

Teacher's notes

Suggested objective: *Explore patterns, properties and relationships.*

Encourage the pupils to experiment with adding and with multiplying. How many relationships can they find?

Name _____ Date _____

Can you find the patterns on a hundred square?

Choose a five by five section of a hundred square.

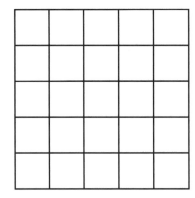

Look for patterns.

Try adding all the horizontals.

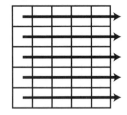

Try adding all the verticals.

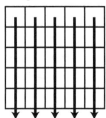

Try adding this diagonal.

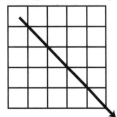

Try adding this diagonal.

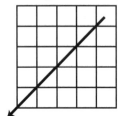

Try adding the sums of the horizontals. Try adding the sums of the verticals.

Try multiplying the centre number by 25 (the number of numbers).

Teacher's notes

Suggested objective: *Explore patterns, properties and relationships.*

Encourage the pupils to experiment with adding and with multiplying. How many relationships can they find? Do they find similar relationships to those they found on the previous sheet?

Andrew Brodie: Maths Puzzles and Games 9–11 © A&C Black 2011

Name _____   Date _____

Can you find the patterns on a calendar?

Here is a page from a calendar, showing the month of July, 2012.

Sunday	Monday	Tuesday	Wednesday	Thursday	Friday	Saturday
1	2	3	4	5	6	7
8	9	10	11	12	13	14
15	16	17	18	19	20	21
22	23	24	25	26	27	28
29	30	31				

Look for patterns. What patterns can you find?

Try looking at a block of 4 numbers:

9	10
16	17

Try adding the horizontals.   Try adding the verticals.

Try adding the diagonals.   Try adding all four numbers.

Try multiplying the upper left number in the block by 4, then adding 16. Compare this answer to your other answers. Do any match? Would this work for another block of 4 numbers?

Try multiplying the lower right number by 4, then subtracting 16.

What if you multiplied one of the other numbers by 4? What do you have to do to find the matching number this time?

Teacher's notes

Suggested objective: *Explore patterns, properties and relationships.*

Encourage the pupils to experiment with adding, multiplying, subtracting and dividing. How many relationships can they find?

Name _____ *Date* _____

Can you find all the rectangles?

How many rectangles can you see in this picture?

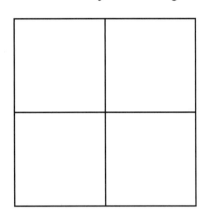

How many rectangles can you see in this picture?

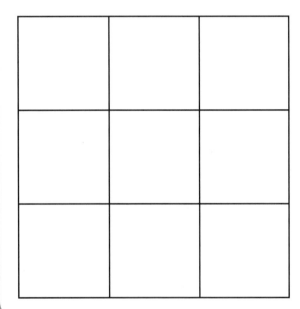

Teacher's notes

Suggested objective: *Identify and use properties of rectangles.*

You may wish to supply the pupils with sheet 63 so that they can experiment with finding the rectangles.

Name _____ *Date* _____

Can you find all the rectangles? Discussion sheet.

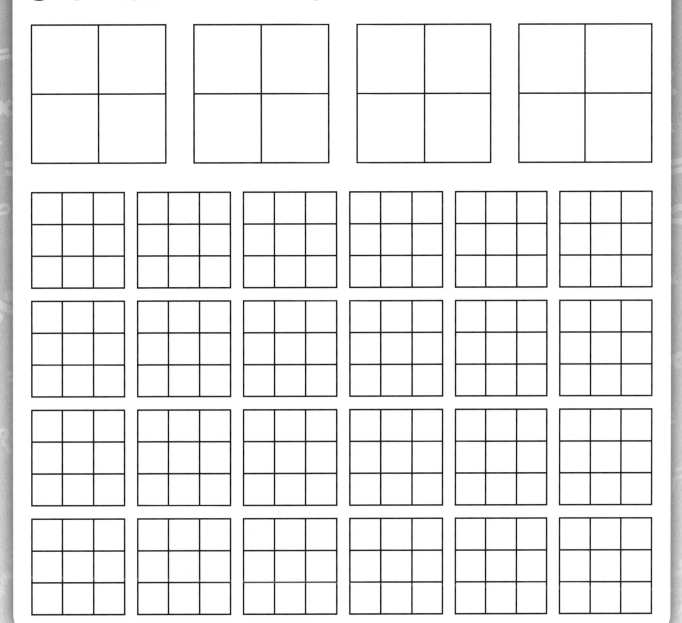

Teacher's notes

Suggested objective: *Identify and use properties of rectangles.*

You may like to use this sheet when discussing all the possible rectangles.

Name _____ *Date* _____

Can you find all the rectangles?

How many rectangles can you see in this picture?

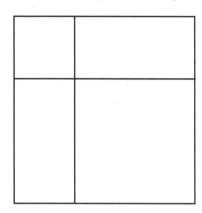

How many rectangles can you see in this picture?

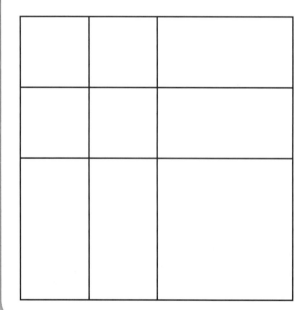

Teacher's notes

Suggested objective: *Identify and use properties of rectangles.*

You may wish to supply the pupils with sheet 65 so that they can experiment with finding the rectangles.

Andrew Brodie: Maths Puzzles and Games 9–11 © A&C Black 2011

Name _____ Date _____

Can you find all the rectangles?

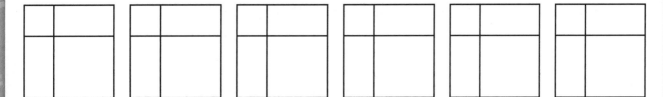

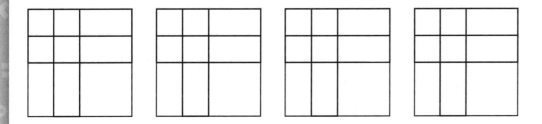

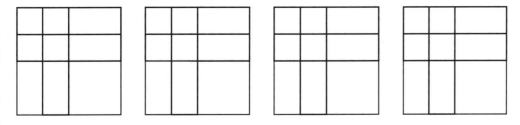

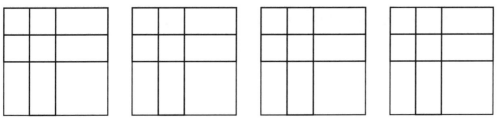

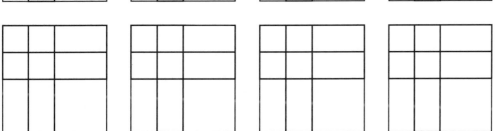

Name _____ Date _____

Who wants to be a millionaire?

A rather clever man was asked to do some work for five days each week for ten weeks. He was told he would be well paid.

"Just pay me one penny for my first day's work!" he insisted. "The next day you can double my pay to two pence."

"Is that all you want?" asked his boss, smiling at the worker's apparent stupidity.

"Well, yes, so long as you promise to keep doubling it every day, I'll work for just one penny on the first day!"

"It's a deal!" said the boss, excited about the cheap labour.

"Promise?" asked the worker. "Do you promise you'll double it every day?"

"Of course I will," replied the boss, shaking his worker's hand enthusiastically.

How long is it before the worker becomes a millionaire?

Teacher's notes

Suggested objective: *Tabulate systematically the information in a problem or puzzle; identify and record the calculations needed to solve it.*

This puzzling problem will challenge the pupils' skills in doubling and in understanding number in the context of money. Ensure that they understand that the question requires them to add all the results until they reach at least a million pounds. The activity can be extended to find out how much the man gets paid on his last day of work. Once they have got over the shock of this activity, they might like to try the next worksheet!

Andrew Brodie: Maths Puzzles and Games 9–11 © A&C Black 2011

Name _____   *Date* _____

Who wants to be a millionaire quickly?

A very clever woman was asked to do some work for five days each week for ten weeks. She was told she would be well paid. She had heard her friend ask for his pay to be doubled each day, after starting with just one penny on the first day. She had also heard the boss agreeing very easily.

"Just pay me one penny for my first day's work!" she insisted. "The next day you can triple my pay to three pence."

"Is that all you want? You're as daft as he is" said the boss, talking about the woman's friend.

"Well, yes, so long as you promise to keep tripling it every day, I'll work for just one penny on the first day!"

"It's a deal!" said the boss, excited about the cheap labour.

"Promise?" asked the woman. "Do you promise you'll triple it every day?"

"I do and I never break my promises!" replied the boss, shaking her hand enthusiastically.

How much sooner than her friend does the woman become a millionaire?

Teacher's notes

Suggested objective: *Tabulate systematically the information in a problem or puzzle; identify and record the calculations needed to solve it.*

This puzzle follows on from the one on sheet 66 and will challenge the pupils' skills in tripling and in understanding number in the context of money. Ensure that they understand that the question requires them to add all the results until they reach at least a million pounds. The activity can be extended to find out how much the woman gets paid on her last day of work – does she ever become a billionaire?

Name _____ *Date* _____

Who wants to be a millionaire very quickly?

Another clever man was asked to do some work for five days each week for ten weeks. He was told he would be well paid. He had heard his two friends ask for their pay to be doubled or tripled each day, after starting with just one penny on the first day. He had also heard the boss agreeing very easily.

"Just pay me one penny for my first day's work!" he insisted. "The next day you can multiply my pay by five to make five pence."

"Is that all you want? You're as daft as they are," said the boss, talking about the man's friends.

"Well, yes, so long as you promise to keep multiplying it by five every day, I'll work for just one penny on the first day!"

"It's a deal!" said the boss, still excited about the cheap labour.

How much sooner than his friends does the man become a millionaire?

Teacher's notes

Suggested objective: *Tabulate systematically the information in a problem or puzzle; identify and record the calculations needed to solve it.*

This puzzle follows on from the ones on sheets 66 and 67 and will challenge the pupils' skills in multiplying and in understanding number in the context of money. Ensure that they understand that the question requires them to add all the results until they reach at least a million pounds. The activity can be extended to find out how much the man gets paid on his last day of work – does he ever become a billionaire?

Andrew Brodie: Maths Puzzles and Games 9–11 © A&C Black 2011

Name _____ Date _____

Who wants to be a millionaire extremely quickly?

Another clever woman was asked to do some work for five days each week for ten weeks. She was told she would be well paid. She had heard her three friends ask for their pay to be doubled or tripled or multiplied by five each day, after starting with just one penny on the first day. She had also heard the boss agreeing very easily.

"Just pay me one penny for my first day's work!" he insisted. "The next day you can multiply my pay by ten to make ten pence."

"Is that all you want? You're as daft as they are," said the boss, talking about the woman's friends.

"Well, yes, so long as you promise to keep multiplying it by ten every day, I'll work for just one penny on the first day!"

"It's a deal!" said the boss, still amazed by his good luck.

How much sooner than her friends does the woman become a millionaire?

Teacher's notes

Suggested objective: *Tabulate systematically the information in a problem or puzzle; identify and record the calculations needed to solve it.*

This puzzle follows on from the ones on sheets 66, 67 and 68 and will challenge the pupils' skills in multiplying by ten and in understanding number in the context of money. Ensure that they understand that the question requires them to add all the results until they reach at least a million pounds. The activity can be extended to find out how much the woman gets paid on her last day of work – does she ever become a billionaire?

Name _____ *Date* _____

Can you work out the additions?

Draw arrows to find the correct sums. The first sum has been done for you.

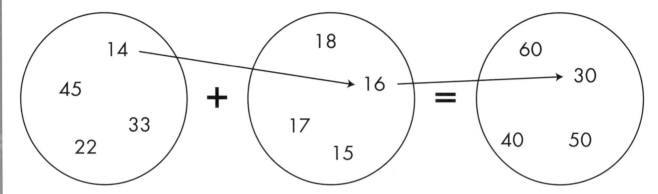

Now try these:

Teacher's notes

Suggested objective: *Explore patterns, properties and relationships involving numbers.*

Do pupils recognise the combinations of units values that result in specific units values, eg combinations that result in a units value of 0, 5 or 3?

Name _____ *Date* _____

Can you work out the additions?

Draw arrows to find the correct sums. The first sum has been done for you.

1.8 0.7 2.5 3.6

+

2.4 2.8 2.3 2.1

=

4.2 3.5 5.7 4.8

Now try these:

2.9 3.2 4.6 5.5

+

8.4 9.8 6.2 8.6

=

14.1 11.3 13 10.8

12.3 15.6 14.7 16.7

+

7.9 6.5 8.7 9.7

=

22.1 23.4 26.4 20.2

Teacher's notes

Suggested objective: *Explore patterns, properties and relationships involving numbers; calculate mentally with integers and decimals.*

Are the pupils confident in addition with decimals?

Name _____ Date _____

Can you work out the subtractions?

Draw arrows to find the correct subtractions. The first one has been done for you.

60 → 16 → 44

70   80   90   —   27   35   42   =   43   48   45

Now try these:

45   95   65   75   —   19   39   29   59   =   26   36   16   56

125   145   205   185   —   99   79   69   89   =   136   66   96   26

Teacher's notes

Suggested objective: *Explore patterns, properties and relationships involving numbers; calculate mentally with integers and decimals.*

Are the pupils confident in subtracting from multiples of ten and multiples of five? Do they see the patterns of results when subtracting numbers with a units digit of 9.

Name _____ *Date* _____

Can you work out the subtractions?

Draw arrows to find the correct subtractions. The first one has been done for you.

3.1 → 1.6 → 1.5

4.3   5.2   6.4

-

2.9   3.3   2.5

=

1.4   3.9   1.9

Now try these:

4.1   6.1   2.1   8.1

-

1.8   2.8   0.8   3.8

=

3.3   4.3   2.3   1.3

5.2   7.4   6.6   8.3

-

1.7   2.8   4.9   4.4

=

4.6   3.9   1.7   3.5

Teacher's notes

Suggested objective: *Explore patterns, properties and relationships involving numbers; calculate mentally with integers and decimals.*

Are the pupils confident in subtraction with decimals?

Name _____ *Date* _____

Can you work out the multiplications?

Draw arrows to find the correct multiplications. The first one has been done for you.

Circle 1: 6, 7, 8, 9
× Circle 2: 7, 9, 6, 8
= Circle 3: 42, 63, 72, 48

Now try these:

Circle 1: 12, 14, 16, 18
× Circle 2: 7, 8, 6, 9
= Circle 3: 112, 108, 144, 84

Circle 1: 15, 25, 35, 45
× Circle 2: 9, 8, 7, 6
= Circle 3: 270, 200, 135, 245

Teacher's notes

Suggested objective: *Explore patterns, properties and relationships involving numbers; calculate mentally with integers and decimals.*

Are the pupils confident with multiplication facts? Can they apply these to numbers that extend beyond the multiplication tables?

Andrew Brodie: Maths Puzzles and Games 9–11 © A&C Black 2011

Name _____ Date _____

Can you work out the multiplications?

Draw arrows to find the correct multiplications. The first one has been done for you.

Circle 1: 6, 7, 8, 9
× Circle 2: 40, 30, 60, 50
= Circle 3: 240, 210, 480, 450

Now try these:

Circle: 12, 14, 16, 18
× Circle: 12, 14, 16, 18
= Circle: 144, 196, 324, 256

Circle: 11, 13, 15, 17
× Circle: 11, 13, 15, 17
= Circle: 121, 169, 289, 225

Teacher's notes

Suggested objective: *Explore patterns, properties and relationships involving numbers; calculate mentally with integers and decimals.*

Are the pupils confident with multiplication facts? Can they apply these to numbers that extend beyond the multiplication tables? Do they recognise square numbers?

Name _____ Date _____

Can you work out the multiplications?

Draw arrows to find the correct multiplications. The first one has been done for you.

Circle 1: 0.3, 0.4, 0.5, 0.6

×

Circle 2: 7, 9, 6, 8

=

Circle 3: 2.1, 3.6, 4.8, 3

Now try these:

Circle 1: 0.4, 0.5, 0.6, 0.7

×

Circle 2: 0.6, 0.5, 0.9, 0.3

=

Circle 3: 0.25, 0.54, 0.24, 0.21

Circle 1: 1.4, 2.6, 3.9, 1.7

×

Circle 2: 4, 3, 5, 6

=

Circle 3: 19.5, 10.2, 7.8, 5.6

Teacher's notes

Suggested objective: *Explore patterns, properties and relationships involving numbers; calculate mentally with integers and decimals.*

Are the pupils confident with multiplication facts? Can they apply these to decimals and numbers that extend beyond the multiplication tables?

Andrew Brodie: Maths Puzzles and Games 9–11 © A&C Black 2011

Name _____ Date _____

Can you work out the divisions?

Draw arrows to find the correct divisions. The first one has been done for you.

Circle 1: 20, 63, 18, 24 ÷ Circle 2: 4, 7, 3, 8 = Circle 3: 5, 9, 3, 6

Now try these:

Circle: 56, 72, 36, 63 ÷ Circle: 7, 8, 9, 9 = Circle: 4, 8, 9, 7

Circle: 64, 54, 44, 84 ÷ Circle: 8, 9, 11, 12 = Circle: 7, 6, 4, 8

Teacher's notes

Suggested objective: *Explore patterns, properties and relationships involving numbers; calculate mentally with integers and decimals.*

Are the pupils confident with multiplication facts? Can they apply these to divisions and numbers that extend beyond the multiplication tables?

Name _____ Date _____

Can you work out the divisions?

Draw arrows to find the correct divisions. The first one has been done for you.

96 → 8 → 12

108   96   ÷   8   4   =   12   27
  120   6   26   20
130   5

Now try these:

140   ÷   7   25   =   20   6
150   30
  160   4   40
180   6

112   ÷   7   8   =   18   17
136   14
  126   9   16
108   6

Teacher's notes

Suggested objective: *Explore patterns, properties and relationships involving numbers; calculate mentally with integers and decimals.*

Are the pupils confident with multiplication facts? Can they apply these to divisions and numbers that extend beyond the multiplication tables?

Andrew Brodie: Maths Puzzles and Games 9–11 © A&C Black 2011

Name _____ Date _____

Can you work out the divisions?

Draw arrows to find the correct divisions. The first one has been done for you.

1600 → 10 → 160

1450   ÷   100   =   14.5

1600   10   145   16

1450   100

Now try these:

2500   ÷   25   =   1.94

1940   10   194

194   100   100

250   100   2.5

800   ÷   4   =   45

900   20   200

640   8   80   90

720   8

Teacher's notes

Suggested objective: *Explore patterns, properties and relationships involving numbers; calculate mentally with integers and decimals.*

Are the pupils confident with multiplication facts? Can they apply these to divisions and numbers that extend beyond the multiplication tables?

Name _____ Date _____

Can you work out the divisions?

Draw arrows to find the correct divisions. The first one has been done for you.

6.4 → 8 → 0.8

4.2

3.6

5.4

÷

8

7

9

6

=

0.8

0.6

0.9 0.4

Now try these:

7.2

6.3

4.8

2.8

÷

0.9

0.7

0.8

0.4

=

6

8

9

7

12.8

12.4

13.5

14.7

÷

2

4

5

7

=

3.1

2.7

6.4

2.1

Teacher's notes

Suggested objective: *Explore patterns, properties and relationships involving numbers; calculate mentally with integers and decimals.*

Are the pupils confident with multiplication facts? Can they apply these to divisions and numbers that extend beyond the multiplication tables?

Name _____ Date _____

Can you identify the correct numbers?

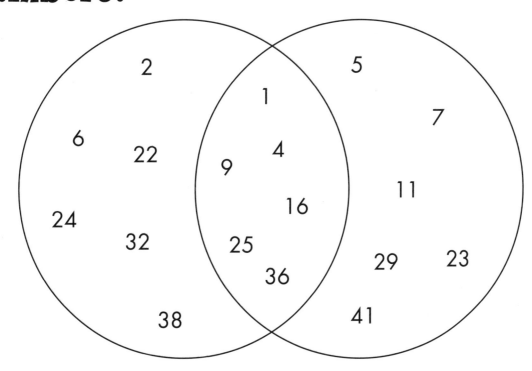

Which numbers are in the right circle but not the left? What is special about these numbers?

_____

Which numbers are in the left circle but not the right? What is special about these?

_____

Which numbers are in the overlap? _____

What is special about the numbers in the overlap?

_____

Teacher's notes

Suggested objective: *Analyse and interpret the data in a diagram.*

Note that this diagram is not a Venn diagram but rather a diagram of three regions.
This puzzle requires the pupils to interpret the wording of the questions correctly.

Name _____ Date _____

Can you identify the correct numbers?

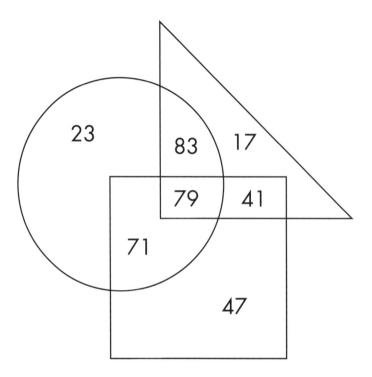

Which number is in the circle only? ▢

Which number is in the triangle only? ▢

Which number is in the square only? ▢

Which number is in the circle and square but not the triangle? ▢

Which number is in the circle and triangle but not the square? ▢

Which number is in the triangle and square but not the circle? ▢

Which number is in all three shapes? ▢

What is special about all the numbers? ▢

Teacher's notes

Suggested objective: *Analyse and interpret the data in a shapes diagram.*

This puzzle requires the pupils to interpret the wording of the questions correctly.

Name _____ *Date* _____

Code	
A	5.6
B	8.4
C	4.2
D	2.2
E	3.8
F	8.2
G	7.2
H	4.6
I	6.2
J	5.4
K	2.8
L	3.6
M	4.8
N	6.4
O	7.6
P	9
Q	6.8
R	8.8
S	3.2
T	3
U	2.4
V	2.6
W	3.4
X	4.4
Y	5
Z	5.2

Can you find doubles to crack the code?

1.7	1.9
3.4	3.8

W E

2.8	4.4	1.9

_ _ _

4.1	3.1	3.2	1.1	3.1	3.2	3.6

_ _ _ _ _ _ _

1.1	3.8	1.2	4.2	1.8	1.9	1.6

_ _ _ _ _ _ _

3.8	4.1

_ _

1.1	1.9	2.1	3.1	2.4	2.8	1.8	1.6

_ _ _ _ _ _ _ _

Teacher's notes

Suggested objective: *Identify the doubles of decimal numbers.*

The children need to double each number provided in the word boxes to find a number to match with a letter. They write the letters found to create the words in a short sentence. The first word of the sentence is 'We'.

Andrew Brodie: Maths Puzzles and Games 9–11 © A&C Black 2011

Name _____ Date _____

Code	
A	3.1
B	1.7
C	2.9
D	4.1
E	2.8
F	3.6
G	4.5
H	3.7
I	4.2
J	3.7
K	3.3
L	4.3
M	2.7
N	3.2
O	4.9
P	4.4
Q	3.9
R	1.8
S	2.3
T	2.6
U	1.4
V	4.7
W	2.4
X	3.8
Y	4.6
Z	4.8

Can you find halves to crack the code?

5.8	6.2	6.4
2.9	3.1	

C A _

9.2	9.8	2.8

_ _ _

7.2	8.4	6.4	8.2

_ _ _ _

7.4	6.2	8.6	9.4	5.6	4.6

_ _ _ _ _ _

9.8	7.2

_ _

8.2	5.6	5.8	8.4	5.4	6.2	8.6	4.6

_ _ _ _ _ _ _ _?

Teacher's notes

Suggested objective: *Identify the halves of decimal numbers.*

The children need to halve each number provided in the word boxes to find a number to match with a letter. They write the letters found to create the words in a short sentence.

Name _____ *Date* _____

Can you move from A to B?

You can only move North, South, East or West, going along the grid lines.

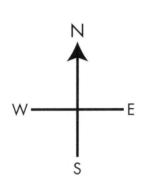

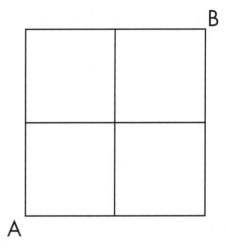

Here are some practice grids.

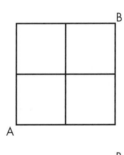
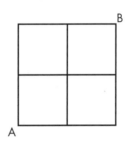
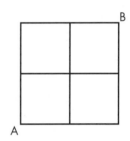

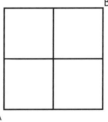
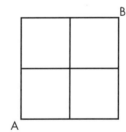
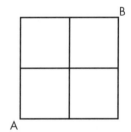

Now experimant with a 3 by 3 grid.

Teacher's notes

Suggested objective: *Interpret patterns and relationships involving numbers and shapes.*

The pupil has to follow the grid lines to find as many routes as possible from A to B. One of the simplest routes would be East 2 steps, North 2 steps; the pupils could show this as: E2, N2.

Name _____ Date _____

Can you get from home to school?

How many different routes are there from home to school?

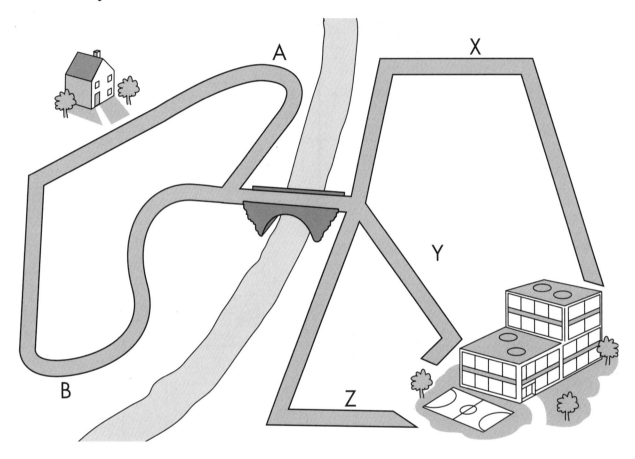

One route can be written as AX. List the other routes in the same way.

If there was another road (C) from home to the bridge and another road (W) from the bridge to school, how many routes would there be now?

Can you find a relationship between the number of roads each side of the bridge to the total number of routes possible?

Teacher's notes

Suggested objective: *Interpret patterns and relationships involving numbers and shapes; suggest and test hypotheses.*

Can the children see the relationship between the combinations of roads and the resulting numbers of routes? They could continue the investigation by changing the number of roads on each side of the bridge.

Andrew Brodie: Maths Puzzles and Games 9–11 © A&C Black 2011